How to Change a
NEGATIVE ATTITUDE

Leslie Parrott

How to Change a

NEGATIVE ATTITUDE

WORD PUBLISHING
Dallas · London · Sydney · Singapore

HOW TO CHANGE A NEGATIVE ATTITUDE
Formerly Plublished as *The Habit of Happiness*

Library of Congress Cataloging in Publication Data

Parrott, Leslie, 1926—
    The habit of happiness.

    1. Christian life—Nazarene authors.   2. Happiness—
Religious aspects—Christianity.   I. Title.
BV450.1.2.P3523 1987   248.4   86-22428
ISBN0-8499-3152-5

98 BKC 987654321

Printed in the United States of America

This book is dedicated to

the people who helped me develop the habit of happiness,
affirm the attitude, and face blind spots in my life.

These include:

Doctors *Ernest O. Milby* and *Walter Johnson*
of Michigan State University,

Doctors *Hardy Powers, Samuel Young,* and *B. V. Seals*
who were ministers extraordinary,

and in a secondary way,
Mr. *Cliff Cowley* and Mr. *Chet Hill*
who proved that pastors,
by their parishioners,
can be taught.

Contents

Foreword

The most important thing about landing is the attitude of the plane." This is what the pilot told me as we were returning home.

My response was an excited, "What did you say?"

When he repeated himself, I said, "I can't believe it! I know the habit of happiness depends on our attitudes. Attitudes affect our relationships. Attitudes affect our moods. Attitudes even affect the way plants grow. But I never knew that a turbo-jet has an attitude."

The pilot, Bob Chenoweth, had landed when he went on to explain himself. "The attitude is down when the nose of the plane is down. And the attitude is up when the nose of the plane is up. If the attitude is too high the plane will come down with a severe bounce. And, if the attitude is too low the plane may go out of control because of excessive landing speed. The trick is to get the right attitude in spite of atmospheric conditions."

This book is about the habit of happiness and how attitudes make or break us. It's about what happens when your attitude is down and what happens when it is up. It is also about what we can do to develop the habit of happiness when the attitude is already down.

This book addresses two questions: (1) Why are there so many unhappy people? And (2) how can we develop the habit of happiness in spite of our circumstances? The book is divided into three parts: (1) Developing the Habit; (2) **Affirming the Attitude**; and (3) **Facing Ourselves**.

There are parts of this book which are autobiographical.

The habit of happiness did not come easily to me. I had to work at affirming the attitude. Other parts of the book are explanations and illustrations of insights on facing the issues of happiness and unhappiness.

The dedication of this book is not made lightly. These seven men (1) at Michigan State University, (2) in the Christian ministry, and (3) on a local church board, constitute the guidance system as well as the support system at strategic points in my development of the habit of happiness.

I am grateful to Professor Larry Finger, whose Ph.D. in English provided the skills and whose friendship gave him the motivation for reading the typescript. I am grateful to Marty Kauffman who transcribed these chapters when they were first dictated. I deeply appreciate the word processing done by Jill Bowling and Joan Bishop in successive rewrites. The final copy was produced by Mrs. Bishop. As usual, I depended on library reference work by Ruth Tomaschke. This book would never be in print if it were not for the encouragement of Mr. Al Bryant at Word, Inc., who edited the manuscript and kept me going with his personal encouragement. Stories have been told in ways designed to protect the privacy of persons involved. But the experiences are all true, as I remember them.

Leslie Parrott
Kankakee, Illinois

PART I

Developing the Habit

Happiness is a habit—cultivate it.

Elbert Hubbard
Epigrams

THE BEATITUDES
Matthew 5:3–12

Blessed are the poor in spirit: for theirs is the kingdom of heaven.

Blessed are they that mourn: for they shall be comforted.

Blessed are the meek: for they shall inherit the earth.

Blessed are they which do hunger and thirst after righteousness: for they shall be filled.

Blessed are the merciful: for they shall obtain mercy.

Blessed are the pure in heart: for they shall see God.

Blessed are the peacemakers: for they shall be called the children of God.

Blessed are they which are persecuted for righteousness' sake: for theirs is the kingdom of heaven.

Blessed are ye, when men shall revile you, and persecute you, and shall say all manner of evil against you falsely, for my sake.

Rejoice, and be exceeding glad: for great is your reward in heaven: for so persecuted they the prophets which were before you.

You cannot read the Gospels without seeing that Jesus did not tell men how to be good in the manner of the moralists of every age, he told them how to be happy.

Sir Thomas Taylor

I can choose to be happy—anyway!

Robert Schuller

1

Happy Anyhow

When Thomas Jefferson included "the pursuit of happiness" among our inalienable rights, he pinpointed two ideas which are important for all of us who want to live out our days with inward joy. *First*, happiness is a process, a pursuit, a way of life. Happiness is a habit. The habit of happiness can dominate all our other attitudes. *Second*, people will interfere with our inalienable right to be happy if we allow them to. If external circumstances determine inward happiness, then our right to be happy can be invaded at any time. However, if our right to be happy is controlled from within, we are in charge. Self-contained happiness is happiness anyhow!

The basic human drive to avoid pain and be happy was consciously alive in me as far back as I can remember. But my pilgrimage toward the habit of happiness (which must exist independent of negative circumstances) did not follow easily. I suffered enough childhood hurts from unthinking adults to make me suspicious. It became easy to be negative toward authority figures during my teen years. My pilgrimage followed a path strewn with the consequences of my own failures. I knew how to have fun, lots of it. But the good times could be obtained only when the external circumstances and the human relationships were nonthreatening. For me to be happy, things needed to be just right. But being happy any-how, from the inside out in spite of negative situations and in spite of people-disappointments, was another matter.

An Italicized Sentence

One of the real breakthroughs in my journey toward the habit of happiness came from an italicized sentence I read in a college textbook—not in a course I was taking, but in one I was teaching.

I have taught the course in "Marriage & Family" in Chris-tian college classrooms and in seminar settings off-campus for years and always with the same basic textbook. Many con-sider *Building a Successful Marriage*, by Landis and Landis, the best text in its field. It has been adopted for use in more classrooms than all the other textbooks on the subject com-bined. And in this highly respected and widely used text-book, written in the usual formal format for college study, there is just one italicized sentence.

"The most important characteristic of a marriageable per-son is the habit of happiness." The truth about happiness in that sentence can be applied to all of us—married, single, divorced, male or female. For instance, "The most important characteristic of a *Christian* is the habit of happiness." Or ultimately, "The most important characteristic of a *human being* is the habit of happiness."

Jesus' Poetic Repetition

Jesus did not use italics. He never wrote any books. But he did have his own ways of making an idea stick. For instance, he was a *master with parables*; and who can forget a good story? He also knew how to use *mental pictures* in ways no one could ignore. Who, for instance, can ever forget the men-tal image of a rich man trying to take his baggage through the eye of a needle?

And Jesus used *poetic repetition* to make an idea stick. The rhythmic repetition of the phrase, "Woe unto you, scribes and Pharisees, hypocrites!" must have been compelling in Jesus' sevenfold denunciation of the scribes and Pharisees (Matthew 23:13–29).

"*Woe unto you, scribes and Pharisees, hypocrites!* for ye shut up the kingdom of heaven against men . . ." (v. 13).

"*Woe unto you, scribes and Pharisees, hypocrites!* for ye devour widows' houses, and for a pretense make long prayers . . ." (v. 14).

"*Woe unto you, scribes and Pharisees, hypocrites!* for ye compass sea and land to make one proselyte, and when he is made, ye make him twofold more the child of hell than yourselves" (v. 15).

"*Woe unto you, scribes and Pharisees, hypocrites!* for ye pay tithe . . . and have omitted the weightier matters of the law, judgment, mercy, and faith . . ." (v. 23).

"*Woe unto you, scribes and Pharisees, hypocrites!* for ye make clean the outside of the cup and of the platter, but within they are full of extortion and excess" (v. 25).

"*Woe unto you, scribes and Pharisees, hypocrites!* for ye are like unto whited sepulchers . . . but within ye are full of hypocrisy and iniquity" (v. 27–28).

"*Woe unto you, scribes and Pharisees, hypocrites!* because ye build the tombs of the prophets . . . ye are the children of them which killed the prophets" (v. 29–31).

Jesus used this same tool of poetic repetition in teaching the disciples the habit of happiness and the need to be happy anyhow: "*Blessed* are the poor in spirit . . . *Blessed* are they that mourn . . . *Blessed* are the meek . . . *Blessed* are they which do hunger and thirst after righteousness . . . *Blessed* are the merciful . . . *Blessed* are the pure in heart . . . *Blessed* are the peacemakers . . . *Blessed* are they which are persecuted . . . *Blessed* are ye, when men shall revile you, and persecute you, and shall say all manner of evil against you falsely . . . rejoice" (Matthew 5:1–12).

Although the sounds of Elizabethan English in the King James Version of the Bible are familiar to our ears, we also know the original word Jesus really used was not the word "blessed," but the more descriptive word "happy."

Jesus believed in the importance of happiness as a habit. When he was ready to teach the disciples on whose shoulders he would lay the full responsibility for spreading the gospel, he began by teaching them how to be happy anyhow. He could have begun his discourse by teaching theology, or the importance of prayer, or the best techniques in personal and mass evangelism. But Jesus began "The Sermon on the Mount" by teaching the disciples how to be happy anyhow: "*Happy* are the poor in spirit . . . *Happy* are they that mourn . . . *Happy* are the meek . . . *Happy* are they which do hunger and thirst after righteousness . . . *Happy* are the merciful . . . *Happy* are the pure in heart . . . *Happy* are the peacemakers . . . *Happy* are they that are persecuted . . . *Happy* are ye, when men shall revile you, and persecute you, and shall say all manner of evil against you falsely . . . rejoice!"

My road toward a continuing attitude of happiness has been something less than a glory-road. Many times I have been unhappy for the wrong reasons, upset over things which were none of my business, and hurt over what appeared to be forays into my affairs which turned out to be more sensitivity on my part than intention on theirs.

A Basic Personality Decision

No one is happy who doesn't make a basic personality decision to be happy anyhow. None of us has the perfect wife. She hasn't been born yet. None of us has the perfect husband. He hasn't been born yet. We can see this by looking into the mirror of our attitudes and behavior. No one has the perfect church. Imperfect members make up imperfect congregations. None of us is the perfect pastor. He has not yet graduated from seminary. During my pilgrimage I have often wished people who bugged me would straighten up and fly right. At that point I still thought my unhappiness was somebody else's fault. But ultimately I learned that happiness was my decision. Until I took responsibility for my own happiness, I was persuaded there was surely a church I could pastor that would make me happier than I was, or at least, less unhappy. Then the idea got through to me that I could be happy anyhow. Happiness, I learned, is from the inside out, not from the outside in. Happiness is a decision, or a lot of decisions one after the other in sequence. Happiness is a habit.

I wish I could say I learned this "happiness anyhow" idea in a flash by reading the Beatitudes, but I didn't. It came as an inner glow which increased unsteadily in my awareness. Then one day, there it was. I saw this whole idea of happiness anyhow, confirmed in the teachings Jesus shared with his disciples in the opening paragraph of the Sermon on the Mount.

The Christmas Story

Can you imagine for a moment how the Christmas story might have been written if Mary and Joseph had not had the capacity to adjust to things beyond their control? To begin with, Joseph did not need an angel to tell him Mary was pregnant. He could see for himself, and the thought of it upset him. Joseph had several options. According to Old Testament law, he could have had her stoned. Or, he may have thought about sending her into some large distant city like Rome, Carthage, or Ephesus, where she could have been lost in the crowd and he would never have seen her again. But Joseph loved Mary, and he did not want to hurt her. You know the rest of the story—how the angel of God came to Joseph and told him that Mary was with child by the Holy Spirit and would give birth to a Son whose name would be Jesus. And Mary and Joseph were married.

To understand the problem of Mary and Joseph, we have to know something about marriage customs in those days. A betrothal was the forerunner of the engagement in modern romances. At the betrothal, the couple was legally bound and could not be separated except by divorce. It could be a matter of years before they were married. And even the marriage ceremony itself covered several days, often as long as a week. Relatives who came ninety miles on the back of a donkey wanted something more than a piece of sheetcake before they returned home! So they stayed around to catch up on family news, build their relationships with each other, and rejoice with the bride and groom. Only when the days of the marriage ritual were ended did the couple begin living together. But they were legally bound from the moment of the betrothal. And with Mary and Joseph, it was sometime after the betrothal and before the marriage that she became pregnant. This called for a major adjustment on his part and hers.

I cannot imagine any couple entering marriage with more problems than Mary and Joseph had. First of all, she was pregnant. There are unrelenting demands for personal adjustments and emotional pressures on a couple during the nine months of pregnancy. And Mary and Joseph were not only waiting for the birth of their first child, they were trying to establish their home, begin a business which must certainly have been undercapitalized, and learn how to live with each other on a seven-days-a-week basis. Mary and Joseph had to cope with all these pressures while continuing to contemplate the meaning of the angel's message about the birth of Jesus. Further, they were forced to close down their business and go to Bethlehem as the first step of a Roman plan to raise taxes. Just what they needed!

I can see Mary and Joseph leaving their honeymoon abode behind them as they went out of the gate of Nazareth early one morning en route to Bethlehem. She was riding on the back of a little burro. No easy ride. I know some women who can hardly ride in a Buick while they are waiting for the birth of a child—let alone on the back of a donkey! Joseph had a short tether wrapped around his arm and anchored securely in his big fist to keep the little brown burro from dislodging

Mary. At night they did not stop in a rooming house or motel as people might today. They stopped along the road, cooked with makeshift arrangements, slept on the hard ground, and made the best of a difficult situation. Even if one has good attitudes the ground can get mighty hard before morning. And Mary was more than eight months pregnant.

Finally, when they arrived within sight of the city of Bethlehem, Mary just stopped. She could not go another step. I can imagine her looking up at her big raw-boned husband and saying something like, "Joe, I cannot take another step. I am going to sit down here under this olive tree, and I want you to go into the city of Bethlehem and get us a room in the Bethlehem Hilton. I would like one in the front if possible so I can watch the crowds go up and down, and I will get room service and wait out the time for the baby to come."

Again we need to understand the marriage customs of those days. Life in the days of the Roman Empire was compressed. A man forty years of age was elderly. Many generals were in their early twenties. And because life was short, couples tended to be married earlier than we think appropriate in our culture. A girl of fourteen or fifteen was marriageable, and at sixteen she would have been considered old. A young man was not married until he was eighteen or nineteen years of age which gave him time to finish his apprenticeship so he could make an adequate living for himself and his wife. So Mary, probably no more than fifteen, was a long way from home, worn out, tired, emotionally drained, and at the end of herself. Furthermore, she must have wondered what she would do if her labor pains began and Joseph had not returned. After all, her baby was almost due. Her anxiety level must have risen as she waited, watched, and eagerly scanned the highway for the familiar figure of Joseph. The teeming crowds paid her no attention.

Finally Joseph returned, his characteristic smile gone. His face was long and the corners of his mouth drooped. She listened as he told her his story: "Mary, I went to the Bethlehem Hilton, but there was no room. It's filled with convention people. In fact, I went up and down the main street to every hotel and motel, but there are no rooms. Finally, I wrenched a promise of space from an old man who has built some new rooms on the front of his place and turned the space out back into living quarters for his animals. It is an exorbitant price, Mary, but he promised me he would clean out the animal filth and cover the floor with fresh straw. And most of all, Mary, he said we could be alone and he would not make us share the stall with any other couple."

I believe she transformed his disconsolate look with her smile of acceptance. "Joe, let's take it." And that night her Son was born.

And that is not the end of the story. A paranoid old king in Jerusalem was beside himself with rage when he learned a baby was born in Bethlehem whom some believed to be a future king. He reacted in the only way an Oriental despot knew. He decreed that all boy babies under two years of age were to be slain. Again, Mary and Joseph were faced with a major adjustment. I can see them again, making their way out of the city of Bethlehem with Mary riding on the back of their donkey. But this time she was holding in her arms the most beautiful gift in all the world. God's only Son, the mind of God who had become a Person, was incarnate in her baby named Jesus. Their flight must have been in the night. I am even sentimental enough to see them riding under a full moon illuminating the Judean hills.

Mary and Joseph were not on their way back to their honeymoon cottage in Nazareth. Instead, they headed straight south across the Gaza strip and down into Egypt not far from the present day Suez Canal. And here, according to scholars, they raised their Son for the first four to six years of his life, while they lived among foreigners who had strange ways and spoke a different tongue.

Mary and Joseph adjusted to many pressure points including early pregnancy, moving, culture shock, and limited finances. All of these problems called for major adjustments if Mary and Joseph were to keep their relationship solid and beautiful. Like every other married couple on earth, they had only one real option: Adjust or self-destruct.

Beyond the Status Quo

Both the textbooks and the Bible make it plain that happiness rests heavily on our ability to adjust to things beyond our control. Since some people are born with rigid personalities (or develop one as they grow up), they find it difficult to change their ways, accept new ideas, or make new friends. Others adapt easily, roll with the flow of events, and lead with their understanding instead of an iron-willed resistance. We all need the courage to go beyond the status quo. Since life requires many adjustments, the person who does not look on change as a threat will make a better go of it than one who does. Maybe that is why Jesus related his axioms on happiness to the *poor in spirit,* those who know how to *mourn,* and the *meek.* These kinds of attitudes suggest people who are both willing and able to adjust themselves to things beyond their control. And to these kinds of people Jesus promised (1) the eternal dividends of citizenship in the kingdom of God, (2) personal emotional comfort, and (3) the earth as their inheritance. The stakes are high but well worth the investment of learning how to accept the inevitable, to place a positive perspective on a negative experience, or to blend our will with somebody else's for the sake of harmony.

Unhappiness is not something we choose. Unhappiness is not a choice but a consequence. It is more like the gray day that comes when the sun doesn't shine. Unhappiness is like the cold mist and fog that fill the valley when the warm earth comes in contact with the cool air. If happiness is the bright sunshine of a clear day, unhappiness is a shadowy existence in the dusk which turns quickly to darkness.

I had always thought we had two options when circumstances leaned against us: the will to be happy anyhow, or the will to be unhappy. However, in seeking the sunshine of happiness to warm our lives, I have about decided we have but one choice, the will to be faithful in following God's ways for working things together for our good. If we fail to make this positive choice, then the dusk of unhappiness moves into place, the temperatures of life's enthusiasm begin to drop, and emotional snowballing covers our relationships. The power of our attitudes to create happiness is frightening, for with it comes the corollary of unhappiness by default.

The Need for Sensitivity

When Jesus' sayings on happiness began to register in my mind, I saw sensitivity in a new light. It all came to me in a sequence of three sayings: "Happy are the *merciful* . . . Happy are the *pure in heart* . . . Happy are the *peacemakers.*" All three—mercy, purity, and peaceableness—are expressions of sensitivity to the needs of others.

Happiness and sensitivity toward others are related. Do you think Mother Teresa, whose entire life is sensitized to the suffering people in Bombay, is happy in her work? I have never met Mother Teresa, but I have seen the connection between sensitivity and happiness at work in a little-known Salvation Army Major in Delhi, India. Major Cook has the care of more than sixty unwanted children, some of them maimed and all of them deprived of any love but hers. With some help from the older children this single woman does most of the work herself in caring for the children and maintaining her quarters. She sleeps with the head of her bed by the door leading into the nursery so she will be awakened by the cry of any of her dozen or more infants. Even in the darkness she can identify each baby by its cry and usually tell what the matter is. Her happiness is an inspiration to all who know her. And somehow I have the feeling that sudden fame through the media would not make her any happier than she already is.

The person with the habit of happiness is more interested in extending mercy than dispensing justice. He finds more joy in forgiveness than in heavy-handed justice. The person with the habit of happiness tends to have open, transparent motives, cleansed and made whole. The person with the habit of happiness is easily entreated, peaceable, and accepting.

This kind of sensitivity does not come naturally in human nature. But there is hope for all of us who want to improve: (1) The Holy Spirit wants to be our Guide and Helper. (2) He will help us find persons who make good models of sensitivity. (3) He will help us further our growth by learning to be friends with people who practice sensitivity. (4) And most of all, we can begin practicing a new awareness toward others and their needs.

Mercy rests on our willingness to forgive. Heart purity is not based on human perfection but on a genuine, authentic, transparent self open toward both God and man. Peacemakers are not disinterested third parties intruding into other people's business. They are people who make it a point to be more involved in solutions than in the creation of problems. Anyone who is dominated by feelings of mercy and forgiveness, who is transparently genuine, and who is a person of peace has already developed the habit of happiness. Mercy, purity, and peaceableness are not dependent on external circumstance. And happiness which generates from within has a better chance to blossom than happiness which always reacts to the social climate.

If we are going to be sensitive toward the people we live with, we need to be aware of the ways sensitivity and insensitivity express themselves. For instance, when I come careening into our driveway, braking to a screeching halt, and slamming the car door behind me as I start up the front steps, does everyone inside relax and say, "It's going to be all right now . . . he's home"? Or do they freeze, wondering what will happen next? If we are sensitive to the feelings of the people at our house, the sounds of our return will generate gratitude. If we have been insensitive we are likely to be greeted with signs of fear and hostility.

I have sat in a board room watching people arrive for the meeting and said to myself as some came through the door, "It will be an interesting meeting tonight!" It did not matter what the agenda contained or what the issues were to be, the presence of certain people always complicated relationships, put pressure on leadership, and usually caused unnecessary conflicts. However, when other people came through the door, I felt like saying, "Thank God. They are here. Things will be better just because they have come." These two different attitudes represent the potentially sensitive and insensitive segments on a church board, in a home, or in any relationship.

In closing this section, let me give a word of encouragement to you if you're caught in a no-win situation. If you live with somebody who bulldozes his way through your feelings to get what he wants, I feel sorry for you. I only know of one thing worse, and that is to be married to somebody who bulldozes his way through your feelings to get what he wants without even realizing he's doing it. If you are caught in this kind of situation, what can you do? You can run, fight, or hide—although each of these options will create new problems. The lesser evil is probably to stay with your situation, but don't roll over and play dead. Instead of being passive and running the risk of self-pity, take charge of yourself. Provide yourself with private time and space. Get out of the house. Create some space which provides relief from the partner who otherwise makes you the victim of insensitivity. Give yourself to a career, to your children, or to some other kind of activity of your own. You are a person and other people cannot destroy your personhood by their insensitivity unless you allow them to do so. It takes a lot of strength and a great amount of courage to do what I'm suggesting, but the price for being victimized by an insensitive person is too much to pay.

Who Touched Me?

While Jesus was walking along the road one day, he stopped suddenly without apparent reason. And turning to his disciples he asked, "Who touched me?" The disciples looked at one another in astonishment. They may even have laughed self-consciously at the idea of trying to identify one person who may have jostled against him in an overcrowded roadway. "Master, there are hundreds of people around. How could we know who touched you?"

But Jesus asked again, "Who touched me?"

Peter, who was almost always the spokesman for any group, may have started to frame a response, "Lord, it's impossible . . . ." His voice trailed off as he realized Jesus would not let the disciples sidestep his question with superficial observations. Jesus asked it again, more in earnest this time, "Who touched me?"

Finally, a frightened little lady came out of the crowd at the side of the road, identifying herself fearfully and self-consciously as the person who had tugged ever so lightly on Jesus' sleeve. The Bible does not necessarily report all she may have said. But her response to Jesus came out of faith born in desperation and symbolized by a touch. She had been sick for years. No doctors had been able to help her. Her illness was undiagnosed. Fearful of annoying the Master, she took the most humble option available to her and reached out to touch him. But the beautiful part of this story is not the fearful touch of the woman but the keen sensitivity of Jesus to both her touch and her need.

None of us will ever be as sensitive as Jesus was. His sensitivity went even beyond the comprehension of his disciples. But all of us can be more sensitive by increasing our awareness of each other's body language. We touch each other in many ways which consciously and unconsciously express our needs. A lingering handshake from a friend, a kiss which is more than a kiss, a stroke on the arm, a pat on the shoulder, or the warmth of a child who curls up at our feet or crawls up on our lap, are only some of the ways we touch each other physically in communicating our needs. The telephone people have helped sensitize millions of family members to the need to reach out and touch each other through long distance conversations. It is even more important to be sensitive to the people we live and work with each day.

The Third Ear

The man who lived among tombs cried out against Jesus: "I did not send for you, who are you? Have you also come here to torment me?" Jesus could have pulled himself up to a full self-righteous height and glowered down at the poor man and cried, "How dare you say such things to me? I just came from the other side of the Sea of Galilee where I performed a miracle and fed 5,000 men, plus all the women and children. They want to make me king. I am somebody over there. And if you think I've got to put up with this kind of treatment, you're out of your mind." If Jesus had talked like that, we would have understood fully because that's the way most human beings react to the icy winds of rejection.

Instead, Jesus responded to the bedeviled man in the tombs the same way Theodore Reik suggests in his marvelous little book, *Listening with the Third Ear*. Jesus did not listen to the words the man shouted. Jesus listened for the feelings behind the words. And while the man was shouting his harsh words, Jesus knew the underlying cry was, "I need help." Most of us can start a quarrel in our house almost any time if we want to take everything everybody says literally. Or, we can develop a sensitivity to the feelings behind the words and respond with our own feelings of understanding. James was right when he wrote, "The wrath of man worketh not the righteousness of God" (James 1:20).

I once saw a training film designed to dramatize what parents do to children which later produces angry adults. In the film the mother and father got at each other through what they said to the little boy. If, for instance, the father responded to the mother because he got a message through something she said to the boy, the mother would shout back, "I was not speaking to you. I was talking to him." In the midst of this emotional crossfire, the therapist pointed out to the mother that she had said something very harsh and unkind to the boy in order to get a message to her husband. But the lady responded, "Yes, but he is too young to understand."

"Yes," the therapist said, "you are right. He is too young to understand, but he is not too young to feel deeply."

The attitudes that make or break a marriage do not surface at the cognitive level of declarative statements but at the deeper level of inner feelings which may or may not be expressed adequately in words. Sensitivity to the feelings of others is not something with which we are born. We are born self-centered and egotistical. We only learn how to deal with other people by intention and practice.

There are specific things we can do to improve our level of sensitivity: (1) We can listen better by concentrating more fully on what people say. (2) We can expand our power for listening by further concentrating on the feelings behind the words. The feelings related to the words are often more important than the words themselves. (3) We may practice empathy (the capacity to put ourselves as completely as possible into someone else's frame of reference, stand in their shoes and analyze the situation as we believe they do). Insensitivity is not inherited through the genes. It is a learned response and can therefore be unlearned through practicing empathy. (4) We can believe that Christ our Lord is both our model and our Source. He will not leave us helpless.

A husband may use his own powerful voice to override his wife's effort to speak. This is a crude technique we learn for grabbing control of the conversation. Or, patronizing one's spouse with false kindness is really a put down which needs to be put out. A lifetime of practicing insensitivity will not be overcome easily. But sensitivity can be learned. And it works wonders in all relationships, but in marriages, it works miracles.

The Jolts of Life

Jesus said, "Happy are ye, *when men shall revile you*, and persecute you, and shall say all manner of evil against you falsely, for my sake. *Rejoice!*"

One of the theories in my world view is that sooner or later, *every man has his own private Gethsemane.* Our Gethsemane will happen in *a familiar place.* With Jesus it was in the place of prayer where he went habitually and where Judas knew he could find him. Our Gethsemane will probably be in our home, on our job, or in the church where we worship. And invariably our *Gethsemane will include a Judas.* Someone will let us down in ways we never dreamed. It may be that our Judas is someone whom we trusted with money. Profit motives are strong in our culture and can sometimes cause a good man to turn against a friend.

Also, in our private Gethsemane there will always be those *close friends who suddenly go to sleep when we really need them*—Peter, James, and John. We may wonder if their telephones have been disconnected. In former times they invited us to go for coffee and we always enjoyed being with them. But now they never call. They find it easier to go down another aisle on their way out of church to avoid our customary place in the sanctuary. They still show up at the usual restaurant but with new people whose presence makes it uncomfortable for us to join them.

A wonderful friend of mine who suffered his Gethsemane in losing a large executive salary told me his big problem was not the money. He could live comfortably on his investment income and the golden parachute the company provided for his big letdown. He said the real problem was the way his closest friends did not know how to act toward him. They tended to follow from afar or ignore him altogether. They did not know what to say, so they said nothing. They just kept their distance.

And finally, in our Gethsemane, we will always see *those who flee in the opposite direction.* They say something like, "Oh, yes, I knew him, but not really. I saw him from time to time, but I really can't get involved in his problems now." And these acquaintances will let us hang when they could have stood up to be counted. Gethsemane will either make us bitter or it will make us better. No one can go through Gethsemane and ever be the same again.

The ability to work through problems is important in marriageability. Almost all problems which confront families have solutions. Unfortunately, many people have never set up a positive system for facing their problems. They do not assess a difficulty realistically. They do not choose ways of acting that will bring constructive results. Instead, they give up easily, consider their situation hopeless, or regress to some form of immature emotional behavior that may create more problems or cause the old ones to snowball to unmanageable proportions. People who face problems realistically and seek intelligent solutions are the most likely to be successful in married living.

Once I saw opposing models of persons dealing with the jolts of life in two families in my congregation. One was a gentleman who was probably the most loved member of the congregation. He never allowed his name to stand for election to the church board. If he had, his election would have been a landslide. Instead, he had a ministry of helpfulness in the parking lot and in the hallways, preferring to be unencumbered with the problems of the official decision makers.

One day when he picked me up at the airport I slid under the steering wheel, pushed down the button which locked all four doors, and said, "Bill, I am not going to let you out of this car until you tell me what happened back there." As a new pastor I had heard bits and pieces but I said, "Bill, I want to hear the whole story from you." Typically, he demurred but then gave in under my prodding.

After working many years as an executive in a national corporation, he took early retirement, turning over his big chunk of severance pay to a Christian friend who had a deal that could not miss. But it did. When I knew Bill he was in his mid-sixties scrambling to live on an inadequate income after his investments had drained away.

Bill was faced with everything the idea of "happiness anyhow" is all about. He had to adjust to things beyond his control, be sensitive to the hurts of his wife who had difficulty understanding what had happened to them, and personally absorb a major jolt. Lesser men have been known to destroy themselves physically or psychologically in the face of problems like Bill's. To begin with he and his wife moved from a big fashionable house to a very small house with a very large vegetable garden. He bought a small economy car in an era when big cars were still status symbols for successful men. When I became Bill's pastor he had moved from behind an executive desk to a street job reading meters for a public utility company.

Bill had every reason to be bitter. Instead, he took his enormous jolt and became a happy man anyhow. I am sure there are people who have been members of that church for ten years and see Bill serving in his several assignments week by week who have no idea he ever suffered a jolt that could have destroyed him. That's happiness anyhow.

In that same church was a woman who sat on the south side of the balcony right by the thermostat. In every service the ushers were asked to adjust the temperature to her needs. The heat or air conditioning were never right for her. She became so obnoxious about her requests that I thought, without ever saying a word, how funny it would be to disconnect the thermostat by her pew and let her change it to her heart's content while we adjusted the temperature from a different control unit on the opposite side of the building. She was unhappy anyhow!

But there were lots of other things this angry lady didn't like. She sent me notes about the hymns, which were all too old or too new, too fast or too slow. If I preached a theological sermon it was "old stuff" and if I preached an updated sermon on human need it was "modernist." Her children were withdrawn from Children's Church at irregular but frequent intervals because people didn't do right. More than once I knelt at the altar in our church, when no one was around, to pray for God to help me treat this lady and her family like everyone else. But she rejected the pastor's love and concern.

One day while I was visiting in her home she relaxed her guard, and in a mellow moment told me her tearful story.

From that day forward, she never bugged me again, for now I understood her. She had a severely handicapped child whom she had kept secreted because of her guilt and embarrassment. The jolt in her life was made more severe by her belief that God had sent the deformed baby as punishment for her sexual sins before she was married. The stress created in the home by a handicapped child is hard and my sympathies go out to any family with a handicapped child. I humbly thank God for three healthy sons. But in this family the jolt was more than they could absorb, and as a result the mother projected all her hurt and frustration on every safe target in her life.

Most of us will never lose our retirement money in a financial scheme with a fellow Christian brother. And most of us will not have a deformed child we perceive as God's punishment. But sooner or later each of us will identify with the human problems included in the words of Jesus: "Happy are ye when men shall *revile* you, and *persecute* you, and shall *say all manner of evil* against you falsely . . . ."

Jesus must have believed we can learn to be happy anyhow because his injunction to us when we are reviled, persecuted, and lied about is to "rejoice." We do not rejoice because of our hard times but in spite of them. This is happiness anyhow!

Discussion Questions:

1. Why is the habit of happiness basic to a good marriage or a good life?

2. Can you think of ways your pastor uses poetic repetition in his sermons?

3. In what ways is happiness a decision?

4. What were the major adjustments Mary and Joseph faced in their marriage?

5. What is the status quo?

6. What is more important, mercy or justice?

7. In what ways can we increase our sensitivity to the needs of others?

8. What does listening with the third ear mean to you?

9. What is the most severe jolt you have suffered in life?

10. What happens when we experience our own private Gethsemane?

Therefore shall a man leave his father and his mother, and shall cleave unto his wife: and they shall be one flesh (Genesis 2:24).

Whoso findeth a wife findeth a good thing, and obtaineth favor of the Lord (Proverbs 18:22).

It is better to dwell in a corner of the house top, than with a brawling woman in a wide house. . . . It is better to dwell in the wilderness, than with a contentious and an angry woman (Proverbs 21:9, 19).

. . . Let the deacons be the husbands of one wife, ruling their children and their own houses well (1 Timothy 3:12).

I will therefore that the younger women marry, bear children, guide the house . . . (1 Timothy 5:14).

Grief can take care of itself, but to get the full value of joy you must have someone to divide it with.

Mark Twain

2

Happiness through Marriage

Most of us have shared in the dream of a happy marriage. The idea of a partnership with somebody we can love, who loves us and wants to share our life, is more than a fantasy. It is a dream most people plan to see fulfilled. We believe that out there somewhere is the one person above all others who can make us happy and with whom we can live out our dream.

Although some of these dreams come true, many of these youthful visions are only partially fulfilled. Others are shattered when the partners wake up to the realities in each other. The happiness in some marriages is finished when the honeymoon is over and the realities of daily living must be incorporated into the relationship. And some dreams of a happy marriage become nightmares. The partnership ends in shambles.

Marriage is a high risk enterprise but people keep on getting married. And marriage breakdowns do not seem to be a deterrent for trying again. Some people continue going for the dream again and again.

Because of the American idea of marriage with someone who has swept us off our feet romantically, there is room for ignorance, misinformation, and poor judgment in one of the major decisions of our lives. A romantic affair often makes people set their judgment aside, forget their moral commitments, and close their eyes to the irreversible, legal, and emotional consequences of a decision to marry. But certainly we should expect to use as much judgment in building our marriage as we do in matters of much less importance.

A Tolerance for Ignorance

People in America have a tolerance for ignorance in matters related to marriage that would not be acceptable in any other area of our lives. If something is wrong with my car I don't want a shade tree mechanic working on it. The complexity of a computerized motor and the sophistication of the electrical system that controls it make maintenance by a factory-trained mechanic a necessity.

If somebody at my house is ill I want a doctor who has had four years of college, four more years in medical school, and four additional years after internship for American Board membership in a speciality. If a doctor has this kind of education and training I will go to him with the person in my family who is ill.

If I have a legal problem I want an attorney who has four years of college behind him, three more years of law school, and has successfully passed the bar examinations to practice law in my state. But even that's not enough for me. I want to know something about his character, his reputation, and whether he can wrap up a legal problem or keep the meter ticking to run up a big bill. When I have satisfied my mind on these matters I will go to the attorney with my property problem or whatever the matter may be.

However, when it comes to the most important area in our lives—love, marriage, sex, raising of children, and all other family matters—everyone is a specialist. No one needs a successful track record in marriage to go on a nationally televised talk show to discuss marriage and family. In this one area of our lives, ignorance is no big liability. All we need for being a specialist in matters of love is personal experience, which may be either good or bad, and our willingness to talk about it. But self-disclosure and self-understanding are not the same thing. There is probably more ignorance about how to build a happy, secure marriage than there is in any other important area of our lives.

The Romantic Myth

We have an idea that the best marriage begins in a romantic affair that sweeps us off our feet. When we experience certain indescribable feelings then "we can know" we have found the right person. At this point young people believe they must quit whatever it is they are doing and get married. If they don't, the two of them will be miserable for the rest of their lives.

I have seen first-year college students drop out of school to get married when they had little beyond the first month's rent. Their education was incomplete. Their career plans were not in place. Their maturity had a long way to grow. These freshman-year marriages are sometimes conceived on the idea that she will work while he finishes college and then he will work while she finishes. And of course it seldom works out like that.

The fact is that marriage decisions for most of the world, for most of its history, have been guided and often dominated by older adults whose marriage and family experience gave them greater perspective and more objectivity than the couple involved. The idea of the young man asking the father for his daughter's hand in marriage is an expression of this idea. Romantic literature and the Hollywood scene have perpetuated the myth of the moonbeam theory of love. The idea that "this love is bigger than both of us" calls for dramatic action even if the action flies in the face of family feelings, parental judgment, and widely shared common sense.

When the idea of a happy marriage is built on romantic feelings, both persons are defenseless before their inevitable disappointments. At the first signs of romance giving way to reality, they sweep doubts under the rug. And when reality finally prevails they get depressed. And when the problems can no longer be ignored, they get on the phone to other people with similar problems and compound each other's ignorance about what really makes a marriage partnership happy.

People of Quality

The fact is that long-term happiness in the marriage depends on the depth of quality in the two people who decide to marry each other. Years ago I pastored a church in a cold climate. It had a parsonage attached to the sanctuary through the church office. Since this church had a disproportionate influence in the community for its size, I had to officiate many weddings for people I did not personally know. And, since my wife could see people come and go through the office she was usually aware of these weddings. When I came back into the parsonage after one of these couples and their family had left, my wife met me with a startling command: "Go in there and spank the boys."

"Why?" I asked her.

She said, "They might grow up and marry some silly girl like that some day."

And I would have to admit that a good gambler would not have put much money on the line, betting on long-range happiness for that particular marriage. The couple were too superficial. There were no signs of depth and little evidence of seriousness about the whole matter. Things that should have been serious, like the exchange of rings, called for giggling. It takes about twenty minutes for a simple wedding ceremony. But it takes years to develop the maturity needed for making the step into a marriage commitment—and years more to let the marriage unfold into a beautiful, secure relationship.

Unfortunately marriage changes only the couple's legal status. Personality is the same after the wedding as before.

An explosive, insensitive, easily angered single man will be an explosive, insensitive, easily angered married man. And a shy, quiet lady who manipulates the men in her life by pouting and withdrawing will be the same kind of person when she is married. Except, after marriage, the negative personality characteristics will be more open and pronounced in both partners since courtship days before marriage bring out the best in people.

A mature, sensitive young man with respect for women will likely continue to mature and develop in the direction his personality is set. And a happy, adaptable young woman with the flexibilities a good marriage requires will likely continue her growth and development long after the events at the wedding have been relegated to the photo album.

Anyone who marries intending to change someone after the wedding is doomed to frustration and defeat. Couples have often asked me to close a wedding ceremony with an addendum that involves three candles in a row on a table. The unlighted candle in the center is taller and bigger around than the lighted candle on either side (these stand for the bride and groom). The bride and groom lift the two smaller candles out of their holders and bring them together so their two wicks make one flame. They then light the larger candle with this single flame, blow out their flames, and place their candles back in their sockets. This leaves the large center candle glowing as a symbol that the two will become one.

We have done the candle ceremony scores of times. But I have never done it without first sitting down with the couple and explaining to them that life doesn't work like that. We don't blow out anybody's personality when we get married. And even after we have been married for ten years, or twenty-five years (or fifty years if we are fortunate enough to live that long), each of us is still our own unique self. Like the snowflake which has many similarities with all the other snowflakes in the same area at the same time, each of us is uniquely different.

A Symptom of Sickness

If any of us is locked into a marriage with a partner who insists on dominating everything, the marriage is sick. I rode once in the back seat of a car and listened to a woman who thoroughly dominated her husband. As we rode along she opened his mail and read it to him, but only the parts she thought he should hear (all the time interrupting herself to give him appropriate directions for driving). "Get into the left lane . . ." And he maneuvered into the turning lane. "The light is going to turn red . . ." And he grunted assent. "Watch that car coming . . . You better speed up . . . Stop . . . Let's go . . ."

After twenty minutes of excerpts from his mail and the staccato instructions on how to drive, I felt like reaching over the back seat to give her a karate chop. Instead, I just looked out the window and felt sorry for a man who had allowed his wife to dominate the details of his life. Maybe he wanted it that way. Or maybe he did not know how, or was unwilling to do anything about it. In any case the results were the same.

The healthy, happy, mature marriage is built on a relationship of mutual respect and autonomy. In the happy marriage each person finds joy in helping the other person develop his or her full potential. It is an imperfect analogy that cannot be pushed too far, but a happy marriage is like a set of rails in a transcontinental railway. Each life parallels the other, rising, falling, dipping, as the journey of life unfolds. Each partner is autonomous, but unfulfilled and incomplete without the other. Conditions change as the journey unfolds but the strength and stability of support for each other never wavers.

The wise old philosopher Pericles stood one day on the steps of the Parthenon on the Acropolis in ancient Greece. He looked down into the valley below (which was Athens), then he lifted his eyes to peer out toward the Mediterranean along the archipelago where, in his imagination, he could see the might and power of the Persian army coming island by island. As he turned once again to look down on the houses of

Athens in the valley below, he said, "I do not fear the might and power of the Persian army from without as much as I fear the spiritual and moral decline of our homes from within." A happy marriage may be enhanced by good things from without but it will be secured from within by the quality of the people who have committed themselves to each other. Outside factors do not destroy happiness in a marriage; immaturity and shallowness do.

Discussion Questions:

1. Why is marriage a high risk enterprise?
2. What joy comes from a happy marriage?
3. What makes a marriage happy?
4. What is one of the first symptoms of a sick marriage?

. . . submitting yourselves one to another in the
fear of God. Wives, submit yourselves unto your
own husbands, as unto the Lord (Ephesians 5:21–
22).

So ought men to love their wives as their own
bodies. He that loveth his wife loveth himself (Ephesians 5:28).

Children, obey your parents in the Lord: for this
is right (Ephesians 6:1).

And, ye fathers, provoke not your children to
wrath: but bring them up in the nurture and admonition of the Lord (Ephesians 6:4).

The supreme happiness of life is the conviction of being loved for
yourself, or, more correctly, of being loved in spite of yourself.

Victor Hugo

3

How to Predict a Happy Marriage

The Terman Building on the campus of Stanford University is a beautiful classroom structure named for a famous professor. Dr. Terman was the kind of teacher every college president and dean tries to recruit. He did not simply teach subject matter, he taught students. He turned on students until they were motivated to do their best. Because classroom size limited the numbers, students competed with each other to be enrolled in his classes.

To predict happiness, or the lack of it in marriage, Dr. Terman did a study of 792 couples, a cross section of America. About one third of them had been to college, some of them had been married less than a year, and others had been married more than thirty years. This meant his study included everyone from newlyweds to grandparents who had already raised their children and were now living as a couple without the children as a buffer between them.

Dr. Terman gave these 792 couples a battery of quizzes, personality inventories, profiles, and other standardized tests. After testing, he brought each of the couples into his office for an interview that began with the same question.

Before I tell you what this question was I want to tell you that Dr. Terman used inductive instead of deductive reasoning. Lawyers use deductive reasoning. If a premise can be established in the minds of the judge and jury, a good lawyer will infer conclusions that seem logical. Abraham Lincoln once got a witness to insist he saw the face of the accused defendant by the light of a full moon. When Lincoln established the premise that his client was identified by a man who depended on light from the moon for his identification, Lincoln brought out the almanac as his authority to say there was no moon shining at the time of the crime. It was an easy step to infer the witness was lying and thereby discredit his entire testimony.

Inductive reasoning is the kind used by scientists in a laboratory. They ask the same question under the same controls until there is no further need to ask it because the answer is always the same. The scientist then infers a general conclusion from the more narrow specific response. Because every loose object drops to the earth, Newton inferred the gravitational pull of mass by earth. Hence the law of gravity.

Perhaps it was the inductive approach which set the final number of couples at 792 instead of 800 or 750. Terman simply asked his question until he did not need to ask it any more. And here is the question he asked each couple:

"By your standards has your marriage been a success?"

If the couple answered "yes" then Dr. Terman learned he could count on certain characteristics showing up in the personality of the woman and another set of characteristics showing up in the personality of the man. The characteristics were consistent and have been confirmed in subsequent studies. Dr. Terman believed, on the basis of his study, that certain characteristics are predictable in the man or woman who will be a good person to live with for the rest of your life.

Kindly Attitudes

The first and therefore the most important characteristic in a woman who will be a happy person to live with is kindly attitudes toward people in general. I must admit this priority about kindness shocked me. I was raised in a culture that proclaimed sexiness and high I.Q. as a woman's best qualities. But Dr. Terman didn't say anything about a Miss America look, or a toothpaste smile, or a set of physical statistics that would make the lady a contender for space on the pages of a fashion magazine. The most important characteristic for a woman who will make a good marriage partner is a continuing regard for kindness. She doesn't have to be good-looking to be a good marriage partner, but she does need to be kind.

I saw the problems unkindness can generate when three couples of us went to visit with a mutual friend who was about to open a new business. I'm sure he had the last minute jitters. And as long-time friends, the purpose of our visit was to reassure him. Through forty-five minutes of friendly inspection, we filled our role, assuring him that everything was beautiful and that the business was a sure success. Actually five of us were supportive while one lady was completely noncommittal. She simply did not say a word. She just clammed up.

Then we came back to the lobby where our tour had started. And there on the opposite wall from the door where we had entered was a sculpture. It was free form, on which we were expected to project our feelings. My simplistic taste in sculpture goes more for human figures or animals. But I did assume this expensive piece of art was selected by a decorator who believed this piece of free form sculpture was just the thing for this business.

Suddenly, the lady who had clammed up and had said nothing, came to life. For openers she started walking to and fro, keeping her eyes focused on the sculpture as she walked. She had everyone's attention. Then she stopped directly in front of the sculpture, spread her legs apart, clinched her fists on her hips, and said in a straight line voice without modulation, "That is the dumbest piece of sculpture I have ever seen." I watched the face of our friend and saw his countenance fall in disappointment and embarrassment. She had been totally noncommittal until there was an opportunity for an unkind remark that cut him like a rapier thrust to the mid-section.

When my wife and I were alone in the car I said, "Thank God I don't have to wake up to that every morning." In her jealous immaturity she had acted like a child when the neighbor kid gets a new bicycle and she has none. The jealous child will throw sand on the bike or find fault with the color. A mature woman who is kind and supportive of people in general has the top quality for a happy marriage.

Expect Kindness

Another personality factor that helps make a happy marriage is a wife who is not only kind herself but expects kindness from others. Most of us receive from other people about what we expect. There is a magical quality about the attitudes we project. Harsh attitudes reap harsh reactions. Kind attitudes reap kindness. The lady who expects people to like her has already sent out unconscious signals that return with the accompanying signs of acceptance. She is invited, included, called, asked, accepted, and appreciated because people find it easy to like her.

Not Easily Offended

The third characteristic in a woman who will make a good life-long marriage partner is an easy way of passing over minor offenses and injustices. Physical pain is a good analogy for mental pain. Everyone has his own threshold of physical pain. Some people, such as professional football players, have a large threshold of pain, and can keep playing the game when the nerves in the body are screaming for attention. Most of us have a low threshold and flinch at the very thought of pain. The sight of a dentist's drill makes most of us rigid and tense.

Just as we all have a threshold of physical pain we also have our private threshold of psychic pain. Some people can take large doses of offense and keep going with a genuine smile. Others of us are devastated by perceived wrongs and incivilities that might not have been intentional. Some people will punish offenders with time in the penalty box for the slightest jostle or kick on the shins that are just the ordinary bruises which happen to people who play the game.

If you are married to a woman who is genuinely kind to all people, who expects kindness from others, and is not easily offended, get down on your knees and thank God for her every day of your life. You are a fortunate man.

Feels Good about Herself

It is wonderful to be married to someone who feels good about herself, who can throw back her head, breath deep, and enjoy life. The woman who is going to be a good life-long marriage partner is not unduly concerned over the impression she makes on others.

Husbands want their wives to look as good as they can, their clothes in style, their hair in order, and their general appearance well groomed. But a woman who becomes obsessed with the impression she makes on others is obnoxious. She is silently repeating the wrong question, "How am I doing?" The woman who is not unduly concerned with the impression she makes on others is in the business of making other people feel at ease. She is more likely to ask, "How are they doing?" She is more interested in making others feel at ease than she is in impressing them.

The Noncompetitive Female

The fifth characteristic Dr. Terman counted on in women who made good partners was their lack of need to keep up with the Joneses. In every relationship, including marriage, there are always the twin factors of cooperation and competition. We like to cooperate with others for the sake of a smooth relationship. But even while we are cooperating, our enlightened self-interest never sleeps and can be activated at any point in the relationship when self-worth is threatened. Since a healthy relationship is based on a mutual ability to enhance each other's value system, the relationship begins to alter when mutuality wanes. Although apathy, disinterest, and antagonism are deterrents to a growing relationship, competition is one of the major factors that put friendships, business associations, and even marriage under stress. A strong competitive woman is not easy to live with.

It takes a lot more grace to enjoy the successes of our friends than it does to comfort them in times of disaster. It takes maturity to genuinely appreciate the achievements among our former college classmates with whom we compare ourselves. It is easy to explain away their higher status and greater success by good luck, inside help, or personal scheming at other people's expense. If another couple's expensive taste in consumer goods turns on a competitive woman, her need to compete can be dead weight in a marriage. Men can be vicious in business competition and on the golf course, while competition among married women is more visible in social relationships. A man who is married to a competitive woman has a tough job keeping up with the Joneses, for about the time they catch up, the Joneses refinance.

The Habit of Happiness

Each of these five characteristics in the woman who makes a good life-long marriage partner is a way of saying she has the habit of happiness. Since the quality of a marriage depends on the quality of the two people who are married to each other it is highly possible to predict a happy marriage. If a lady (1) is critical and unkind, (2) thinks people don't like her, (3) is easily offended, (4) is obsessed with the impression she makes, and (5) is competitive in social relationships—you can count on it, she will be hard to live with.

Happiness in marriage is just the flip side of these negative characteristics. You can predict a good marriage with the woman who (1) is kind to everyone, (2) expects kindness from others, (3) is not easily offended, (4) is not unduly concerned over the impression she makes on others, and (5) does not see social relationships as rivalry situations. This kind of woman has the habit of happiness. All five of these characteristics are attitudes and we have the power to control them.

Aren't these characteristics unnecessarily hard on the wife? Don't men need these same five qualities too? The answer is "Yes." These characteristics are *human* qualities needed in all of us. However, when applied in marriage they are what makes a woman a great partner. And the qualities that make a man a good husband are needed by all of us. However, in the context of marriage these qualities are manly. If a man is going to be an above average risk as a life-long marriage partner he will (1) have an even and stable emotional tone, (2) be basically cooperative with his wife and family, (3) have equalitarian ideals toward women, (4) have benevolent attitudes toward the underprivileged, (5) and be unself-conscious and somewhat extroverted.

Emotional Tone

The most important characteristic in a good husband is an even and stable emotional tone. I must confess this shocked me when I first read it. The media would make us think a man worth marrying ascends the ladder of desirability on the rungs of power and money. According to popular wisdom, a rich business man is a better catch for marriage than a truck driver. The rich man can provide more things money can buy than the working man. But both the business man and the blue-collar worker may have the even temper and emotional stability that make them good marriage partners. Or, their uncontrollable tempers and emotional instability may make either of them a disaster to live with. There is nothing inherent in the extremes of wealth and poverty, high status and low status, or power and weakness, that delivers an even and stable emotional tone.

An uneducated friend of mine has raised five children with apparent success. His children, for whom he sacrificed to give them all good educations, have all the evidences of sound marriages, good career choices, and consistent attitudes of happiness. When I asked him how he did it, he tried to side step my question with a light-hearted rejoinder. But I pushed. I said, "My wife and I have been watching your family closely and we just wish we could be sure our three boys will turn out as well as yours already have. And I want to know. How did you do it?"

Finally, he responded, "I am not sure. I may be wrong but I think success in raising children has more to do with the character of the father than it does the mother." Then he said something that made me laugh until I saw he was not laughing. He said, "I think a kid who has a dad who is mad all the time has a better chance to grow up and amount to something than a kid with a dad whose emotions are on a yo-yo and the kid never knows what to count on."

As though I had not heard enough already, my friend wrapped up his answer with a third observation. "A kid with an unstable dad follows a pattern: He will play or hunt with his dad, but never quite trust him. After school he will play around until his dad arrives home, then take a reading on his mood, and adjust himself the best way he can. A child who is developing into an angry young man has a lot of years to build up resentment. When the boy is about sixteen or seventeen years old he will tear your heart out!"

An angry teenager gets even by turning against his family's values. He may not have the courage to attack his father directly, for he stands to lose too much. But he will reject with a vengeance whatever the father believes in. If the father loves the church, he will turn against the church. If the father is a physician and wants his son to be a doctor, the boy will reject medicine as a career. If the father is frugal, the boy may very well be a spendthrift. These are the ways an angry teenager gets even.

Much of the home and family literature these days focuses on the importance of a good man in the household. One-parent families are more likely to have an absent father who is unstable and poorly adjusted emotionally than an absent mother with the same characteristics. God never called men to be economic and political conquerors of their little worlds. But he did call them to be the salt of the earth, to be like a city set on a hill by which other people may measure their journey, and like lamps on lampstands in homes that are more cozy and secure because they are there. The husband with an even and stable emotional tone is off to a fast start on the way to happiness through marriage.

Basically Cooperative

The second characteristic of a man who will make a good husband is the desire to be cooperative with his wife and family. Some men's first response to anything their wife and family want to do is resistance. In essence they say, "No, I'm against it. Now you convince me." Let me give you the case of an imaginary family picnic:

When the family suggests a picnic in the park the father comes on with strong resistance. He justifies his negativism with reminders of problems on other similar outings. The kids made too much noise in the car. The good tables were all gone when they arrived. The bugs were bad. Somebody forgot the salt for the hard-boiled eggs, and on and on.

To win his cooperation, the wife and children combine promises with concessions. The little children promise not to make a sound in the car all the way out and all the way back. The father wrenches a promise from the children even God knows they cannot keep. Children have never been put together for silence in the back seat of a car headed for a picnic. But since they have promised to be still, he is justified to yell and slap them around when they do what children usually do. And if he wants to spiritualize their back seat noise he can say, "You lied to me because you promised to be still."

After the family has promised to send an older boy out on a bike ahead of time to sit on a good table, get flypaper for the bugs, and salt for the hard-boiled eggs, and so on, the father at last relents and the picnic is on its way. Like a good union negotiator, the father gets the commitments up as high as possible before he clinches the deal. And with his non-cooperative approach he places all the responsibility on his wife and family while he holds on to the full authority by which they will be judged. If anything goes wrong—even if the weather turns bad—he can say it is their fault for he didn't want a picnic in the first place and only gave in to make them happy. This kind of man inflicts lots of pain on a marriage partner while a man who is basically cooperative becomes a one-man support system that brings happiness.

In the administration of a happy enterprise, responsibility and authority go together. Things begin falling apart when authority and responsibility are separated. If a man is given a job and is not given the commensurate authority to get the job done, it won't be long before he resigns. If the man with responsibility and limited authority can't resign for need of the pay, he will settle into a defensive mode that results in limited productivity, uncreative solutions to problems, easy irritability, and chronic fatigue. And this kind of worker will bad mouth the source of authority at every opportunity.

The principle of combining authority and responsibility works in marriage. The man who tells his wife to dress well and gives her no freedom with their money has given her responsibility without authority. The cooperative husband, on the other hand, finds his happiness in helping his wife achieve her purposes. Cooperation does a lot toward holding a marriage on course.

Equalitarian Ideals

Happiness through marriage is further increased by partnership with a man who believes in equalitarian ideals for women. I am not talking about women's lib or the Equal Rights Amendment as causes. However, I am talking about the openness of a man to accept his wife as a fully franchised member of the partnership with serious consideration for her ideas and feelings, and responsibilities and authority equal to her skills and interests. I believe this concept of equalitarian ideals begins with a husband's willingness to listen.

During all the years our boys were growing up I took my wife to lunch at least once each week. We chose lunch because the children were in school and because we could afford lunch better than dinner. Although these lunch times were planned for me to hear her agenda, it was not easy for me to learn how to listen to my wife. I tended to jump to what I thought was going to be her conclusion. I was often wrong. I tried to speed up her side of the conversation by telling her I was more interested in her conclusion than in her process. She let me know I could not understand the conclusion if I didn't listen to the process. So much of what she had to say reminded me of quotes, or anecdotes, or chapters from recent books I had read. However, all of my ready fund of raw material that I thought was a contribution to our conversations was more like an intrusion that impeded the process of learning to listen. I finally came to realize that ministers talk more than they listen. It's expected. But little by little she taught me, and I learned, how to button down my tongue so I could listen to what she said, and even more important, what she was trying to say. We moved away from Portland, Oregon, in 1970 when I became a college president. But in all the visits back, the places my wife wants most to go to are some of those restaurants where we had lunch and I learned how to listen to her.

During the years we lived in Boston we had a place on the coast of Maine at York Harbor. One of the many good things about Maine is the Fisherman's Walk which separates the roaring, foaming ocean from the property of private owners. In the old days the Fisherman's Walk was provided by law so men who had lost their gear in a storm could use this walkway to retrieve their buoys and lobster pots. Some of the fondest memories of our years in Maine are tied to our conversations as we walked hand-in-hand up and down the Fisherman's Walk talking and listening, and learning together. Equalitarian ideals begin with the willingness to walk and talk and listen together. God came down in the cool of the day and walked and talked with Adam and Eve in the Garden of Eden. And when their relationship with God was broken, Adam and Eve hid from God and did not respond to his voice. The process of alienation and separation was in motion.

The man with equalitarian ideals toward women will encourage his wife in developing her gifts and skills. This willingness may involve a wife's own job or career, but not necessarily.

After conducting three funerals in ten days for men who died of heart attacks in their forties, I came suddenly to realize how little many women know about their family finances. None of these three widows had any concept of money and one of them told me she did not even know what bank her husband used.

For more than twenty years I had done the banking, paid the bills, and balanced the checkbook at our house. I mistakenly thought this was a husband's job. But in one of our luncheon conversations I accepted the fact that women live longer than men and with my schedule and temperament, my wife's life expectancy is probably much greater than mine. Maybe it was a moment of weakness, or great inspiration, when I looked across the table at my wife and said, "Why don't you take over the family finances and manage our money?"

I was a little shocked when she responded with enthusiasm. "I would like that very much."

We went to the accounting firm of Arthur Anderson,

where one of our friends was a vice president, and explained our decision to him. He got out a set of books and showed my wife how to keep her accounts. And from then until now she has been in charge of our financial affairs including the annual itemized report to the Internal Revenue Service. Her sense of self-worth rose several points when she took over this financial responsibility, and her level of confidence has increased with the passing years. Each year, when we visit our tax accountant, I am proud to hear her discuss figures with authority.

I am by no means suggesting that all husbands should turn over the family finances to their wives. That might be a disastrous move in some cases (but perhaps no more so than is already the case with the husband keeping the books!). However, I am suggesting that ways must be developed to help fulfill the equalitarian ideals in a marriage partnership. Unfortunately this cannot be done unless the husband really believes his wife is fully an equal with him.

There are three areas of decision making in a marriage: (1) By mutual understanding there are decisions that call for the husband to take the lead. (2) There are other decisions that call for the wife to take the lead. (3) And there are some decisions that cannot be satisfactorily made unless the partners talk out the issues involved and make a joint decision. This is how family leadership is likely to be delegated and implemented in a marriage relationship based on equalitarian ideals.

A Reason for Gratitude

If you are a woman married to a man (1) with an even and stable emotional tone, (2) who is happily cooperative with you and the family, and (3) is committed in practice to equalitarian ideals in marriage, you are a fortunate wife. You have a reason for gratitude. Your marriage relationship is a long way down the pike toward the habit of happiness. But no man can fulfill these ideals completely. Success in the quality and character of these attitudes is in degree. Success is in the direction the marriage is going, not in the destination.

Benevolent Attitude

The fourth characteristic of a good husband is a benevolent attitude toward the underprivileged and those of lesser rank. Servicemen have an uncomplimentary word for officers who salute their superiors and kick their inferiors. There is a personality disorder in a man who "shines the boots" of those he hopes will reward him and is uncivil to people he considers safe targets. The attitude a man has toward the underprivileged, who are not likely to reward him, and the socially inferior, who may not have a way to strike back, is a strong indicator as to how he is likely to treat his wife and children.

Happiness in marriage involves fulfillment through positive relationships between the partners. This is especially true with a wife. Even a healthy relationship with a good boss on the job, or a positive pastor in the pulpit, or a helpful married brother can compensate minimally for a negative relationship with a nonsupportive husband at home. But in the marriages husbands and wives jointly described as successful, the husband had good attitudes toward the people he could possibly hurt and get away with it. A man who loves children and accepts all people as his equals will find it easy to demonstrate love for his wife by attitudes and behavior patterns that support fidelity.

Unself-conscious and Extroverted

Don't put down the husband who laughs loudest at his own jokes. The quiet, silent type may be weak instead of strong. It is hard to know for sure. At least you have an idea about what is going on in the mind of the man who talks big and laughs loud. No man needs to be the "life of every party" to be a good husband. But studies have shown that men who can talk easily and laugh at themselves are much more likely to have an acceptable level of self-disclosure and thereby be better husbands than the men who use television to escape interaction.

I was a guest at the Sunday dinner table with a pastor and his family that included a three-year-old who sat on a stack of phone books so she could reach her plate. At a quiet point during the meal the little girl in her high, sweet voice said, "Daddy, now it's time for you to tell your two jokes." The father was disconcerted and embarrassed. But I insisted he tell his two jokes, which really were funny. It may seem corny for a father to have a repertoire of two jokes that he tells with enough predictability for a three-year-old to learn his timing. But it is still better to be married to a man with two jokes than a man with no jokes.

A Summary Word

All five of these characteristics that make a man a better than average risk as a marriage partner are attitudes. And every man controls the way he thinks. There is no reason to be afraid of happiness in marriage with a man (1) with an even and stable emotional tone, (2) who enjoys being cooperative, (3) who believes in equalitarian ideals, (4) who is benevolent toward the people less able to help themselves, (5) and who tends to be unself-conscious and somewhat extroverted. This kind of man will be good to live with because he already has the habit of happiness.

When Marriages Turn Sour

We have spent most of this chapter talking about the qualities that usually exist in marriage partners who see their relationship as a success. However, there were characteristics, according to Dr. Terman's study, that reflected the personalities of the people who felt their marriages had not been a success. There were three reasons at the top of the list: (1) selfishness, (2) complaining, and (3) lack of affection.

The unhappy husbands often saw their wives as only loving the children or only interested in their own families and seeing the husband as a convenient means of support. Unhappy wives often saw their husbands as primarily interested in their fishing buddies or golfing partners and only using them as objects of sex and dependable housekeepers.

Complaining was another matter unhappy married people talked about. Each thought the other was unreasonable in their demands, and hopeless beyond reach in the things they complained about. One woman who lived with a complainer told me she determined many mornings that she would be careful all day to avoid anything that would give her husband grounds for complaining. "But," she said, "we would not be through breakfast until something I did was wrong and we were off to another of our unhappy days."

And, unhappy couples often talked about the lack of affection. And anyone who cannot give affection finds it hard to receive affection. This sets the marriage relationship on a very physical, mechanical base that becomes more unsatisfactory as time passes by.

Given these three types of unhappy attitudes, any marriage in time will end in civil or psychological divorce. If sanctions or other concerns such as church, family, or children keep a couple legally married, they can still suffer the pain of psychological divorce. They may live under the same roof but never have the happiness through marriage that God intended when he organized the world into families at the beginning of human existence.

Discussion Questions:

1. What is the most important characteristic of a marriageable person?

2. What is the main characteristic of a woman who will make a good marriage partner?

3. What is a threshold of offense?

4. What is the first characteristic of a man who will make a good marriage partner?

5. What does it mean for a man to have equalitarian ideals toward women?

And Joseph saw Ephraim's children of the third generation . . . brought up upon Joseph's knees (Genesis 50:23).

. . . Visiting the iniquity of the fathers upon the children, . . . unto the third and fourth generation . . . (Exodus 34:7).

Bless the Lord, O my soul, and forget not all his benefits: who forgiveth all thine iniquities; who healeth all thy diseases; who redeemeth thy life from destruction; who crowneth thee with loving kindness and tender mercies; who satisfieth thy mouth with good things; so that thy youth is renewed like the eagle's . . . . But the mercy of the Lord is from everlasting to everlasting upon them that fear him, and his righteousness unto children's children (Psalm 103:2–5, 17).

The promise is unto you, and to your children (Acts 2:39).

And he took a child, and set him in the midst of them: and when he had taken him in his arms, he said unto them, Whosoever shall receive one of such children in my name, receiveth me; and whosoever shall receive me, receiveth not me, but him that sent me (Mark 9:36–37).

The hardest habit of all to break is the habit of happiness.

Theodosice Garrison
The Lake

4

Growing Up Happy

I have often wondered if the sin that can be passed to the third and fourth generation is related to negativism from which the habit of unhappiness grows. Parents can teach negative thinking to their children who then transmit the virus to grandchildren and great-grandchildren. There is ample evidence that unhappiness runs in families. Neurotic mothers often have neurotic daughters. Angry men may have angry sons, and unhappy parents may have unhappy children and grandchildren.

But there is evidence that the habit of happiness also runs in families. When Paul chose Timothy for the ministry he said, "I thank God . . . that I may be filled with joy; when I call to remembrance the unfeigned faith that is in thee, which dwelt first in thy grandmother Lois, and thy mother Eunice; and I am persuaded in thee also" (2 Timothy 1:3–5).

Years ago Norman Vincent Peale submitted a manuscript to his publisher on the subject of faith. He explained with many examples how the power of faith could change men's lives by changing their outlook. At one point the editor, Myron Boardman, had a conference with Dr. Peale on the proposed title for the book and the meaning of the word *faith* as Dr. Peale used it. To the editor it was obvious that faith has different meanings for different people. Myron Boardman finally asked Dr. Peale, "Aren't you talking about faith as a power of positive thinking?" The manuscript was edited using Dr. Peale's idea of faith as positive thinking, and the title was changed to *The Power of Positive Thinking*. The book not only became a best seller; it made the idea of positive thinking a household term in America and in much of the world.

The faith Paul saw in Timothy was without doubt the Christian faith founded on belief in the Resurrection of Jesus. But I have no trouble believing that the faith Paul saw in Timothy as a third generation Christian also included the power of a positive outlook. I believe Eunice had the habit of happiness, a habit she helped her daughter Lois to learn. And Lois transmitted the habit of happiness as a way of life to her son Timothy.

All of us who have children, or who think about having children someday, are concerned about how we may help them grow up happy.

The Old-fashioned Family

Many believe the habit of happiness would grow naturally in children if the old-fashioned family could be restored as a bulwark of love and security. Everyone has his own memory of the old-fashioned family, but many see it as a home where father made the living and mother strove to become a model homemaker. Everyone did his chores. In the evening they all gathered for a family dinner. In many homes without servants, father dried the dishes as mother washed them, while the children turned to their homework with the older children serving as tutors for the younger ones.

In the old-fashioned family the home was the center for everything really important. The best eating place in town was at home. There were close ties to the church and the school. Recreation centered in the home, not in a facility at the school or church where a specialist was hired to supervise. There were no counseling centers. Every family had its therapy of work, play, and shared wisdom. There were few divorces because of economic dependence on each other. In the farming community the man needed a good wife. A wife depended on her husband for support. Children needed their parents and parents needed large families to do all the work on the farm. Economically they were dependent on each other.

But anyone who is trying to maintain this ideal of the old-fashioned American family today is fighting a losing battle. The agrarian society of small towns and family farms is not what it used to be. The automobile and the assembly line have irreversibly changed the direction of our culture. The flow is now to metropolitan centers where each member of the family has opportunity for economic independence and individual autonomy. Secularism, peer pressure, and mobility are important words in understanding the modern family.

The state of the family has changed drastically in the last two generations, but the personal needs of the family members for love and security have not. Food stamps, government subsidized housing, and Social Security function as programs in a safety net legislated to give every family some security for its physical needs. But there is no way to legislate responsibility for providing children with love, emotional support, defense against disruptive outside forces, and good parental models who practice the habit of happiness.

Charlie Shedd said, "The best thing I can do for my children is to love their mother very well." He is right. However, if Charlie Shedd and his wife are models of happiness for their children, it is not because external authority requires it. Transmitting the habit of happiness to the next generation is a matter of making love work in spite of the changing family. Divorce, drugs, one-parent families, multiple marriages, and the tendency toward social irresponsibility among teens are facts to live with. There are no pat answers or quick fixes in helping children develop the habit of happiness. But there are clues, suggestions, and guidelines that may prove helpful.

Love As a Compensating Factor

Not many adults have had the ideal childhood. A hostile neighborhood, disruptive school problems, broken homes, alcoholism, unsatisfactory church relationships, and physical disabilities are just a few of the factors that may impede the growth and development of the habit of happiness in a child.

If there is anyone who should have rebelled against the values of mother and dad, I should have. From my earliest days in grade school, I lived for the time when I could take lessons on a horn and become a member of the marching band in the local high school in Springfield, Illinois. I tried to start lessons in the fourth grade, but the teacher said my lips were not yet well enough developed. At the beginning of the fifth grade, I started taking lessons with enthusiasm, practicing daily, and participating with success in all of the zone and state instrumental contests open to public school pupils in Illinois. Finally I finished the eighth grade and was looking forward to entering high school and playing in the marching band the next September. I had already been accepted and had shifted my concern from band membership to winning first chair in the French horn section. Then, one day during the late summer, my father came to talk with me in a serious way that made me know I would not like what he was going to say. He tried to soften the news, but the abrupt truth was, "Les, you cannot play in the high school band."

I still do not understand why two very influential women in the church my dad pastored had a vendetta against the high school band. It may have been that one of them lived opposite the football field and was frustrated with the noise high school students created on Friday evenings in the fall. The other lady was even more irrational in her stand against "the theater," a concert hall where the band held its widely publicized and highly successful annual spring concert. Her strong feelings against the appearance of evil included her pastor's son being in the band that played in a theater.

My father explained patiently that he did not agree with

these women and even though they were dead wrong he would pay a big price to go against them. They had the capacity and the will to create havoc in the congregation. And the best way to avoid the havoc was for me to stay out of the marching band. Acquiescing, I went across the high school campus to play first chair French horn in the orchestra, not the band, hating every minute of it. On the way home from school, I often paused by the band building to listen and watch through the windows as they created the musical sound that made me wish I were one of them.

In later years I saw how the love and concern of my dad and mother brought me new experiences that replaced my dream of playing in the high school band. They bought me season tickets each year to the local concert series that featured the great musicians of the world. It never dawned on me until years later why my dad always dropped me off for the concert and came back to pick me up when it was over. Mom and dad did not have enough money to buy tickets for both of them and me.

I well remember my father driving our family from Springfield to St. Louis, where we attended the open air light opera. My sister and I had the best seats in the house. I was not so much interested in what happened on stage as I was in the music that came out of the orchestra pit. And from where I sat, I could actually look over the rail and see the music scores on the lighted stands of the players. In those days the opera managers arranged for people to come in after the performance began and stand, free of charge, at the back of the open air arena on a space available basis. I can hardly write about it without becoming emotional, for I vividly remember turning around in my seat during the overture and seeing the profiles of my mother and father against the evening sky as they stood there taking up free space while my sister and I enjoyed the best seats in the house.

As I look back on those days, it seems to me now that no family ever had more picnics, more vacation trips to grandmother's house in Nashville, more fishing trips, and more of the other kinds of family events than we had. I know now what I did not know then: that dad was compensating for the severe disappointment I experienced in not being able to play in the marching band.

All families have their problems in helping children develop the habit of happiness. In many households it is easier to be negative than to be happy. But in every family there is one parent or both parents who can practice the principle of compensating love. It goes a long way in helping children overcome the pull of gravity toward negativism and setting them free to be happy.

The Magic in Unconditional Love

In many ways my wife and I have had an ideal marriage and an ideal family. We married early and learned how to live happily by maturing together. We started our family after eight years of marriage, which gave us a lot of time with each other before the first baby was born.

We wanted boys and God gave us three of them, healthy and bright. The two older boys are Eagle Scouts. The youngest boy has enjoyed the usual advantages of a third child who came along after his brothers were already in school. We promised the boys we would pay their tuition as long as they went to school until they got doctor's degrees, even if they were married. All three have taken us up on our promise, which we have scrambled to keep. They are married. And their careers are in the early developing stages. Most important, they all, including their wives, practice a vital Christian faith in harmony with our own. Their habit of happiness is genuine.

But in a home like ours, which we thought was providing the boys with all they needed, we suffered a close call. I want to tell you the story and suggest it could happen to anyone.

When we got ready to have a family we thought we had a great idea in planning for two children close together. This would make it possible for them to be playmates, look out for one another on the playground, and in general, grow up with companionship. The only thing we forgot was sibling rivalry. Every child with brothers and sisters is afraid the amount of love mother and father have to give is not sufficient to meet the full needs of each child. Therefore, some children compete with their siblings to get their full share of parental love. That competition, which shows itself in a hundred ways, is called sibling rivalry. And at our house we had it wall-to-wall with two sons only twenty months apart.

The older boy, typical of first sons, easily internalized the value system of his father. He became a good student, earning the continued approval of his father by writing good papers, getting high marks on exams, and keeping a good grade point average year after year. When he was only a child, he had no fear in reciting the Christmas story to several hundred adults or reporting to a Sunday morning congregation on a Holy Land trip he and I had made. He went through college with grades that got him ready acceptance into graduate school. And at one point, two of his teachers, at separate times, wrote me letters about the quality of his term papers.

But the second son, less than two years younger, looked at his brother's success in academia as pure competition, decided to reject the whole idea, and refused to compete. He turned to athletics. He played football in high school and soccer in college. For three successive summers, he attended a boarding school for tennis players at Carlton College. But all the time, his grades were those of a gentleman, or not quite that good.

He and his brother were following the prototype of the elder brother and the potential prodigal. Like other parents, we always gave the oldest son greater responsibility and commensurate authority. When the two children were sent off together, we said to the older son, "Here is the money. You take care of it. And watch over your little brother, and don't let anything happen to either of you." The "little" brother, only twenty months younger, looked at all this display of trust in someone slightly older, with whom he felt equal, and his teeth were set on edge. When they got home and the report of some problem was high on their agenda, we listened to the younger child as he stammered and stuttered, trying to tell what had happened, his mind going faster than his tongue. Finally we stopped him and, sitting him down, turned to the older boy, just twenty months his senior, and said, "Now you tell us what really happened." A decade of this kind of unconscious, deferential treatment by his mother and me resulted in an angry eleven-year-old second son who chose to act out his frustration by reacting against school.

Time and again, week after week, I set him down on Thursday night and drilled him on his spelling words until he could spell each one of them correctly and use the word accurately in a sentence. Then he would go to school the next day, miss half the words, and come home to show me his paper with no apparent feelings of remorse or sense of failure. I did what I thought every good father should do. I spanked him. But it did no good. Then I spiritualized the problem, and prayed with him. He was not impressed with my prayers. Then I tried to buy him with the promise of expensive gifts if he would learn to spell, but his needs were all met anyhow, and he was not moved by my materialistic brand of motivation.

Finally, one day in a flash of insight I realized that the behavior pattern I would have identified in a moment in any other family I had not recognized in my own. I really don't know why this analysis of the problem was so slow in coming. But when it came, it hit me like a harpoon. I took my wife to lunch and explained what I thought was happening. Our second son was trying to tell us in a hundred ways that he did not want to be his older brother's little brother. He did not want his older brother to be his keeper and he did not want me to love him because he spelled correctly but because he was my son.

It was almost Christmas, and I was getting ready to leave on Christmas Sunday evening for three weeks in Germany on a speaking assignment. We did not have the money, so we borrowed it from the bank and bought our eleven-year-old a ticket to go with me. We put the ticket in a box and placed it under the Christmas tree. He shrieked with excitement when he opened his present and saw what it really was. And on Christmas Sunday night he and I left on a nonstop flight from Portland, Oregon, to Kennedy Airport in New York City, the first leg of our overseas journey.

Although this journey was going to change both our lives, it started out low key. I made up my mind I was not going to push him to talk with me. I would wait until he was ready, whenever that might be. I just read my book, slept, made superficial remarks about the flight and the meals, and waited for time to do its work. We came in over New York at daybreak. In those days the pilots were allowed to circle Manhattan to give the passengers a spectacular view of those great concrete canyons. In my own excitement I blurted out, "Wow, that is really something, isn't it?" He responded with a noncommittal sound that was really no word at all.

For three days I thought he really was not going to talk. Then suddenly, without any provocation, he started to babble like a brook. We talked hours on end about anything and everything. One morning I woke up in a little hotel in Salsburg, Austria, and he was sitting in a chair by the side of my bed waiting for me to open my eyes so we could talk. In those days a good Chateaubriand could be served in your hotel room in Europe for a small amount, and we caught on to the system quickly. Each night we would enjoy our lovely meal in the privacy of the room—while we continued to talk, talk, and talk. Until this day, Rog and I still refer to places we visited on that trip, places where national news often focuses its cameras.

Finally we were on our way back home, flying across the North Atlantic. It must have been about 3:00 in the morning when everybody else on board was asleep except Rog and me—and we were talking, well, Rog was talking, in the dark. Finally I said, "I'm concerned about this spelling business."

Like a flash, he shot back, "Oh, Dad, don't worry, I'll take care of it."

I did not even respond. And that brief exchange was all the discussion we had on spelling during the entire three weeks we were together.

Back in New York, I put him on a nonstop flight for Portland while I went on to Kansas City for some church business that brought me home some days after he had arrived and had taken his first spelling test. Never, not one more time, did I drill him on Thursday nights. I disciplined myself not to talk about spelling except on Fridays when he brought his test scores home. And for thirteen consecutive Fridays, without me drilling him or making any kinds of threats or promises, he had perfect scores on all his spelling tests.

Poison in the attitudes of a perfectionist parent can inflict children with negativism and the habit of unhappiness that may dog their steps the rest of their lives. Every parent cannot be fortunate enough to have three consecutive weeks with his son or daughter in a setting that gives the child undivided attention. But somehow, somewhere, parents like myself, with tendencies toward perfectionism, need to analyze their expectations and find ways to make love work because the child is my child, and not because my child makes me look good by being a high achiever.

Loving the Neurotic

Of all the unhappy people in the world none suffers more than neurotics. They are the result of a system that produces unhappiness. Somewhere in the developmental process neurotics are derailed. At critical times and places in childhood there is no one to help them, and they don't know how to help themselves. No one in their support system understands the principle of compensating love. No one in their family knows how, or takes the time, to develop the self-confidence that will help make them grow up happy. It may or may not be their own fault that they grow up to be unhappy neurotics.

The question is, "Are they stuck?" Is there anything to be done for the chronically unhappy person whose miserable future is guaranteed by his free-floating anxiety and consistent distortion of reality?

There is hope. But hope for the neurotic depends upon the availability of some person God can use as the conduit for his unconditional love.

I have a friend who went to a state mental institution as an intern during his final year in seminary. When he arrived the psychiatrist in charge was unprepared for the student's coming. He saw the seminarian as the last straw in a work load that was already overflowing. Exploding in the student's face, he said, "I don't know why they send you young men up here. You don't have any medical training to do these people any good. It is a waste of the taxpayer's money and a waste of my time, and it really doesn't help you."

But after his tirade, the psychiatrist finally said, "Well, you are here, and there is nothing I can do about it. If you will go down that long hallway to the very end room, you will find a twenty-bed ward. And in the far corner of the ward is a woman who is going to be there the rest of her life. You can't do her any harm, so why don't you go down and talk to her?"

With this kind of negative send-off, my friend went down the long gray corridor of the state hospital, found the large ward, and located the lady in bed number 20 in the farthest corner. He pulled up a chair by her bed and sat down. She did not move, even to open her eyes. He began slowly. "I am not a doctor. I have not come to make any tests. In fact, I probably cannot do you any good. But I do want to get acquainted with you and tell you a little about myself. And I thought maybe you might like to tell me something about yourself." He continued talking quietly in a reassuring tone of voice as completely nonthreatening as he knew how. For some time the lady in bed 20 continued to give no sign of recognizing his presence. But then slowly she turned toward him with searching eyes. After an hour of uncertain encounter, he excused himself and was gone.

The next day the young seminarian returned to bed 20. Before his hour was up, the patient began to speak cautiously, mostly asking questions. He came back again on the third and fourth days. And on the fifth day he closed his hour by telling her, "I will not be back tomorrow. I am going to a little church where I serve as pastor." And as he looked at his watch, he said, "At about 20 minutes after 11:00 o'clock on Sunday morning, I want you to think about something. We call the people of our congregation forward to kneel around the altar for a time of family prayer. And, I am going to tell them about you. They will pray for you, and beginning right then, many of them will start to love you even though they have never seen you. I want you to think about this, and think about us while we are there on our knees praying for you." With that he dismissed himself, and was gone.

The young preacher came back the second week, and the third week, and finally the second month, and the third month. On his last day of internship he told the lady in bed 20 he would not be back anymore. "I am going back to the seminary to graduate. I have already been appointed the full-time pastor of a congregation, and my wife and I will move to this new church immediately. However, I want to promise you one thing: my wife and I will pray for you every day of our lives. And, if you will write me, I promise to answer you on the same day I receive your letter or card." And he was gone.

After more than a year of letters and prayers, the young man and his wife went back, on their day off, to the community where the big hospital was located. He was walking down the main street of the little town when suddenly he looked up and saw before him, coming on a direct line, the psychiatrist who had treated him with unnecessary harshness. He told me that his first impulse was to duck into the drugstore and hide behind the Hallmark cards. But the psychiatrist saw him. It was too late to run. Coming with a quickened pace, the psychiatrist greeted him with arms extended. The doctor pumped and pumped his arm while he exploded in a big smile and a happy, "Nice to see you." It was no ordinary handshake. And finally when he let go of the minister's hand, the doctor went on to say how glad he was their paths had crossed for he had something to tell him. He said, "I need to apologize for the way I treated you. I am sure I was exhausted and saw your coming as one burden more than I could handle at the time. I hope you will understand. But," he said, "I want to tell you about that lady in bed 20.

"I would have been willing to put my career on the line that she would have spent the rest of her days in the hospital. But after you left, something very wonderful and strange began to happen. She experienced remarkable improvement. In fact, she did so well emotionally we gave her a weekend pass. The weekend at home was a success so we gave her a second and a third. And now she has proved to us that she can go home and live a normal, happy, life with her family. I don't think she will ever be back in the hospital again."

A neurotic is a chronically unhappy person, an emotional cripple, bogged down in their pilgrimage but not without hope. The dramatic story of what happened to the lady in bed 20 is an example of what can happen in less severe cases if there is someone available as a conduit of God's unconditional love. Stern lectures delivered in anger are not therapeutic with unhappy people. But love that works in a nonthreatening way has the touch of divine magic.

Discussion Questions:

1. What characteristics of the old-fashioned family can we still retain?
2. How is love a compensating factor?
3. Is unconditional love really possible?
4. What hope is there for the neurotic to be healed?

In the year that king Uzziah died I saw also the Lord sitting upon a throne, high and lifted up, and his train filled the temple. Above it stood the seraphim: each one had six wings; and with twain he covered his face, and with twain he covered his feet, and with twain he did fly. And one cried unto another, and said, Holy, holy, holy, is the Lord of hosts: the whole earth is full of his glory. And the posts of the door moved at the voice of him that cried, and the house was filled with smoke. Then said I, Woe is me! for I am undone; because I am a man of unclean lips, and I dwell in the midst of a people of unclean lips: for mine eyes have seen the King, the Lord of hosts. Then flew one of the seraphim unto me, having a live coal in his hand, which he had taken with the tongs from off the altar: and he laid it upon my mouth, and said, Lo, this hath touched thy lips; and thine iniquity is taken away, and thy sin purged. Also I heard the voice of the Lord, saying, Whom shall I send, and who will go for us? Then said I, Here am I; send me (Isaiah 6:1–8).

Behold also the ships, which though they be so great, and are driven of fierce winds, yet are they turned about with a very small helm, whithersoever the governor listeth. Even so the tongue is a little member, and boasteth great things. Behold, how great a matter a little fire kindleth! And the tongue is a fire, a world of iniquity: so is the tongue among our members, that it defileth the whole body, and setteth on fire the course of nature; and it is set on fire of hell (James 3:4–6).

Confess your faults one to another, and pray one for another, that ye may be healed. The effectual fervent prayer of a righteous man availeth much (James 5:16).

Since habits become power, make them work with you and not against you.

E. Stanley Jones

5

Learning to Listen to Ourselves

During the height of the Watergate scandals people never met for coffee at the counter of a local cafe or appeared on a nationally televised talk-show without shifting the conversation from wherever it began to a discussion of the bugging of the White House. Even the comedians could not ignore what the President had done. I heard one of them say the President of the United States had honored the occasion of the birthday of the Vice President by sending him twelve long-stemmed microphones.

But through all this turmoil with accusations and counter-accusations, White House statements followed by disclaimers, and confusion heaped on confusion, there was one question that kept coming into my mind which I could not escape. *"Les Parrott, if you bugged yourself, what would you hear?"* What would my conversations for a day or a week reveal about the habit of happiness? Does the great body of conversation in daily experience fortify the habit of happiness or obstruct it?

If it were possible to record everything each of us has said in the last year and then run these tapes through a computer, we would all know if happiness is a habit of ours or only a sailboat in a sea of negativism. Some people enjoy expressions that need a snarl along with the words. A smirk on the face or a curl of the lip come naturally with certain combinations of words. Other people can talk about the same situation or the same people, using adjectives that are soft instead of harsh and words that smile instead of snarl. One person's choice of words ameliorates stress while another person's use of words compounds it. Happiness is what we say and how we say it!

No exercise I know about can be more useful in helping us understand our attitudes better than taking time to listen to our own conversations. Each time we are able to dominate a conversation, we usually turn it to one of a handful of subjects that preoccupy us. We take over conversations like cars coming out of the cloverleaf onto the freeway. When we anticipate somebody's need to stop for a breath, we take over the conversation by beginning to talk with an enlarged voice at an accelerated pace. Like drivers on the freeway, we make the other people move over or slow down while we dominate the lane. And each time we lead the conversation, it follows the well-defined limits and guidelines of all our former conversations. These repetitive themes, forever dominating our conversations, are always colored with a positive or negative emotional tone. If we could listen to ourselves, we would know that happiness is what we say and the way we say it.

Listening to a playback of our conversations really makes sense if we are interested in identifying and improving our attitudes. At the time of the Watergate hearings, we had a boy at our house who thought bugging and listening were good ideas. Halfway through an evening meal, I heard an electrical sound—beep . . . beep . . . beep . . . beep— coming from underneath the dining room table. The beaming twelve-year-old slid off his chair and disappeared underneath the white linen tablecloth to reappear in seconds holding a small tape-recorder that I recognized as my property. Then I watched him as he traced a cord from that tape-recorder underneath his plate to the center of the table where my wife had arranged a floral centerpiece. He triumphantly lifted a concealed microphone from among the flowers and announced proudly that he had recorded the first half hour of our table conversation. This was bad enough, but then he insisted we listen while he played back all the things we had said to him and to each other in the half hour. At first it was funny and then we all got more serious. Finally we became defensive as we tried to explain that we didn't mean things like they sounded.

In the third grade I read the myths attached to the life of Paul Bunyan, the legendary woodsman from the headwaters of the Mississippi River in Minnesota. He was larger and more powerful than any other man in the woods. His voice caused the birds to stop singing and the leaves to tremble. Everyone did what he commanded them to do, that is, with the exception of one man. One woodsman was given to streams of profanity and blasphemies which scandalized the usually unimpressed ears of the other lumbermen. Paul Bunyan's command for him to stop using his obscenities did no good. Bunyan then did the next natural thing. He thrashed him. But that did not stop the flow of bad language. Paul Bunyan begged, cajoled, threatened, bribed, and otherwise called on every means he knew to stop the terrible bursts of expletives, but to no avail. Then something happened that changed everything.

One winter it got cold enough in Minnesota to send the mercury in the thermometer through the bottom of the ball to unmeasurable degrees below zero. The extreme cold instantly froze each word as it was spoken. Watching these frozen words drop to the ground gave Paul Bunyan an idea. He ordered all of the frozen words of the offensive lumberman to be picked up and stacked in successive order waiting the coming of spring. When the bitter cold of winter gave way to the warming rays of the sun and the temperatures began to rise above zero toward 32 degrees and on into the melting zone, Paul Bunyan made the lumberman sit down and listen to every expletive he had uttered all winter. And according to the story, the man never swore again. If Paul Bunyan could talk I'm sure he would agree that it makes a lot of sense to listen to what you've said and how you said it.

The Paul Bunyan story is myth, but the report I read on the potential for retrieving words that are still floating around in the universe is not. Some scientists say that technological breakthroughs may make it possible to reach out into the air and pull in speeches and conversations that set airwaves in motion hundreds or even thousands of years ago. Theoretically, the words of Abraham Lincoln's Gettysburg Address, or the Beatitudes in the Sermon on the Mount are still floating around in the airwaves. Impossible as this idea sounds, it is both magnificent and frightening. Many things are said, even on public occasions, that are better forgotten. Moments of passion evoke words of insensitive disregard. However, words have a life of their own. Once spoken, they can never be unspoken. I am sure these scientists who talk about bringing back words from the past would agree that it makes a lot of sense to listen to what we have said and how we said it.

According to motivational theory, there are only two kinds of managers, those who are motivated primarily *to achieve,* and those whose first concern is *to keep good relationships.* Each of us is a combination of both of these motivations until a moment of truth arrives and decisions have to be made that either come down on the side of achievement or conciliation. I know a manager whose employees and friends would agree that he is highly motivated to achieve. He watches the bottom line, talks a lot about profit and loss, pushes the production line, urges haulers to load their rigs and move on out.

Some time ago he told me something that turned up the amps in my attention meter. He said he went into his office every Saturday morning when the place was silent, the watch dogs were back in their kennels, the secretaries had gone, and even maintenance men were off duty. And there in the stillness of the total managerial situation, he sat at his desk and played back to himself all of the conversations and relationships he had experienced during the past week. Then he went on to tell me that it was not uncommon for him to phone somebody with whom he had exchanged strong words during working hours or to meet a colleague at the country club for lunch to reconcile their differences.

When I asked him why he did this playback routine (since the company was his and he was only accountable to himself), he said, "I just know myself well enough to be aware that I will step on toes when I need to in order to get the job done. But I never want any negative emotional hangovers from the previous week charged against my relationships which begin again each Monday morning." My manager friend has learned that it makes a lot of sense to listen to what we have said and the way we said it.

Bugging did not begin with the hi-tech recording systems of Richard Nixon, the Kennedy brothers, or Lyndon Johnson. The idea of bugging was not original with Franklin Roosevelt either. He cut a hole in the floor under his desk, for his secretary to sit in a chair on a table below. Unknown to the visitors she took notes on important conversations. But long before the tape recorder and the plastic disc, 750 years before Christ, a twenty-year-old man named Isaiah learned the meaning and the power of listening to himself. His world was disintegrating. The king (who was loved and respected) had died of a lingering disease. His son's ascension to the throne was a national disappointment.

To understand the moods and the actions of Isaiah, we need to remember what young adults are like. People in their early twenties are in the most idealistic period of life. These are the people who join the crusades, set out to correct the social and political mistakes of their parents' generation. Young Isaiah, the age of most college sophomores, saw every national indicator on social justice turning downward. In those hard times they suffered their own counterparts of high unemployment, double digit inflation, and skyrocketing interest rates. The international scene was equally dismal. The *Jerusalem Morning News,* if there was one, had just run a story on Jezebel, who had terrorized a vineyard owner as the means to secure his land. Visitors from the north told horror stories about her destruction of cherished traditions, her use of the powers of the monarchy for personal privilege, and her forced changes in the religious habits of the people. And the threat of a Judean invasion by eastern armies was more than speculation.

But in the midst of all of this turmoil and confusion, Isaiah went into the temple to worship. Apparently they sang their version of the hymn that went, "Holy, Holy, Holy, Lord God Almighty." Prayers went up like incense to fill the open spaces above the heads of the worshipers. And here Isaiah stopped, sat down, and began to listen to himself. And what he heard, he did not like. Finally, young Isaiah cried from the depths of his depression, "I am a man of unclean lips, and I dwell in the midst of a people of unclean lips."

"Unclean lips" did not mean Isaiah was a man who used expletives that should have been deleted. I doubt he cursed and blasphemed God. I think it meant his overwhelming sense of helplessness and discouragement in the current scene came out in a flow of negativism. Since Isaiah dwelled in the midst of "unclean people," he was surrounded by negativism. His support group, such as the people he might invite to his place for a social evening, were those who shared his same prejudices and frustrations. And, as they sat about, sipping and munching and talking, they reinforced each other's negativism. Isaiah was negative and all his friends were negative, too.

But something unusual and unexpected suddenly happened in the temple. God sent an angel carrying "a live coal in his hand which he had taken with the tongs from off the altar." The angel touched the lips of Isaiah. The heavenly visitor who was God's representative could have touched Isaiah's mind or his heart, but instead he laid the live coal on his mouth. And with the purging of his lips, young Isaiah's life was changed. Isaiah was like the rest of us. His tongue was the catalyst that changed the rest of his life. With the purging of his lips, his life took on the quality of a mission. "Here am I, send me" were the words from Isaiah's lips, which launched him on a career spanning sixty years as counselor and spiritual guide to the kings in the palace at Jerusalem. And Isaiah, whose life was transformed by a change in attitude, also became the author of one of the most beautiful and powerful prophetic books in the Old Testament.

The best way to know ourselves is to sit down and play our conversations back to ourselves. If we can identify (1) the subjects we talk about most often, (2) the attitudes we invariably invest in these conversations, (3) the kinds of positive and negative words we choose most often to express ourselves, and (4) the character of the nonverbal communication we choose to accompany our words, we will know whether we have a set of attitudes working for us or against us. A change in the basic flow of words from negative to positive begins with the will to listen to the way we talk. For those who are willing to bug themselves and take what they hear seriously, there will be wonderful results.

As a Man Speaks

If we listen to ourselves, we can identify our real values and priorities. We talk most about the things that matter most in our lives. "As a man thinketh in his heart, so is he" is not an empty saying, but truth with a difference. And another inspired word may be added, "As a man speaks, he reveals to us what he really cares about."

I called a friend halfway across the United States to confer with him on a problem. As soon as my friend realized I was on the other end of the line, he started in with an enthusiastic report about all the things he was doing in his job. He talked about numbers, bottom line, future options, strategies, problems, and on, and on. Finally, I interrupted him, "This is my nickel! I called you!"

He said, "I know. But I want to tell you one more thing," and away he went again. Finally I hung the phone back in its cradle and turned away from the desk toward my wife who was standing in the doorway of the study.

She asked, "What did you learn?"

And I answered, "I learned what he really cares about."

Halfway across the United States on long distance with me paying the bill, my friend talked about the things that were high on his own agenda. In our conversations we fail to talk about the things that are important to us because other persons have their agenda of concerns. In conversations we compete to see who will choose the topic and how long we can keep our topic up front.

I usually fly tourist class. I would fly third class if there were one. However, I did fly first class on a recent flight between Chicago and Seattle with tickets supplied by the people for whom I was going to speak. The forward cabin of this Boeing 747 was resplendent with large, beautiful seats, efficient hostesses, and a bountifully spread buffet on a linen tablecloth. I had never seen a buffet on an airline before. Enjoying the unaccustomed luxury, I stood to let my wife into the aisle so we could walk to the buffet. Just then, a man whom I had never seen before in my life tapped me on the shoulder from behind and stuck out his hand to greet me. He was a big, affable fellow in a golf sweater, smiling and talking to me like we were friends.

Our conversation was not small talk about the weather or when the plane would land in Sea-Tac. Within a matter of seconds, he began telling me all of the important things in his life. He gave me his name. He let me know that he had just retired from a job in Chicago with a company that had honored him at a big retirement dinner the night before and had given him a gold watch. He did not like the dinner, the gold watch, nor the young man they introduced to take his place. Then he started talking about the illnesses of his wife who was momentarily in the washroom.

Finally, he whipped out the pictures of his grandchildren and told me how his daughter and grandchildren would meet him at the airport in Seattle. And last, his face clouded as he

told me that he did not know what he would do after he finished visiting with his daughter, for he had never really made
any plans for retirement. He just hated the whole idea. And
there, in a matter of three or four minutes, this new friend told
me everything that was important to him. By this time the line
moved forward and our conversation was cut short by the serious business of selecting food from the buffet.

I had never seen him before, and I probably will never see
him again. But, like every other human being, including me,
he predictably talked about his own private agenda. I might
have tried to tell him about my concerns if our conversation
had not been aborted by the demand of choosing the hors
d'oeuvres.

Some years ago a group of social scientists at Duke University got the idea that they could understand relationships in
families more fully if they could listen to the unrehearsed
conversations of families at dinner. Arrangements were made
and the table talk of families in the research group was
recorded over a six-week period. One of the most interesting
results of the study was the description of the hierarchy of
table conversations:

First were the families who had nonconversations. They
spoke in monosyllables, "Meat . . . bread . . . beans
. . . ," as their needs arose. For these families, eating had
very few social overtones. They concentrated on food, ate
fast, and left the table as soon as they were satisfied.

*Second were the families whose conversations were pre-
dictably critical.* They criticized the menu, the way things
were cooked, and how they were served. Parents disciplined
the children at the table. They lectured them sternly and
sometimes struck them, seemingly unaware of how inappropriate the family dinner table is for meting out punishment.
According to the researchers, these family conversations often ended in tears with somebody running out of the room
and slamming the door.

*Third were the families who had enough ego strength to be
supportive of each other but thought the rest of the world was*

primarily inhabited by fools. They genuinely believed that tearing down someone else helped to lift up themselves. The President of the United States, the gas station attendant, and the school teacher were near the top of their unending list of stupid people. Their worst jibes were reserved for the authority figures in their lives. Conversation around these dinner tables was a running commentary on life from a negative perspective.

Fourth were the materialistic families. Their conversations focused on their possessions and those of others. Their secularism often included emotional involvement in professional sports. They were sophisticated consumers of all that a superficial life could offer. Their concerns were an inch deep and a mile wide. The center of gravity for their self-worth ran through their bank account. Their ability to buy was the barometer that set the level of their happiness.

And finally, at the top of this five-step hierarchy, were those families who used dinner time to talk about ideas and issues. Their agenda included current events, recent books they had read, anecdotes on the political scene, and concerns for social action. Their humor was genuinely funny and not thinly concealed barbs designed to hurt someone else's ego.

Years ago, while our family lived in Boston, I became intrigued with the Kennedy family. Since my assignment involved flying between Washington, New York, and Boston, it was not uncommon to see one or more of the Kennedys on board. Once while we were waiting in the aisle for the door to be opened, I asked young Joe Kennedy why he had a canvas knapsack over one arm and a sleek, expensive leather briefcase in the other hand. Turning on the contagious Kennedy smile and pointing toward the knapsack, he said, "This is for when I do my thing . . ." and holding up the briefcase, he said, "And this is when I do their thing." There is no doubt the Kennedys had a deep-seated sense of responsibility for public service. "Their thing" and "my thing" were closely related.

When I realized that each of those sons and daughters of Ambassador Joseph Kennedy was endowed with a $10,000,000 trust fund that became payable on their twenty-first birthday, I wondered why they did not all become social drop-outs. Although I have read all of the books on the Kennedy family I know about, the last one I read gave me a partial answer as to how the Kennedy children were first motivated for public service. In *The Kennedy Women* Pearl Buck says the Kennedy family followed a tradition of always having a full family dinner served at the main dining table on evenings when the father, Joseph Kennedy, was home. Presiding at the head of the table, the father strictly enforced ground rules on conversation. They never talked about money. They never criticized another Kennedy. And finally, they were urged to talk about issues and ideas, particularly political issues and ideas. Sometimes the Ambassador assigned the children homework that prepared them for the next family discussion of ideas and issues. This kind of family dining may be far too structured for most families. But teaching the children to talk about ideas and issues apparently paid off.

Basically Positive or Basically Negative

Everything we put into our mental computer comes from one of five sources: hearing, seeing, smelling, tasting, or touching (plus the possible addition of the sixth sense of intuition). But just before we put any sound, sight, smell, taste, touch, or intuition into our computer, we exercise a God-given authority to stamp it with a bold imprint that says "positive" or another bold imprint which says "negative." Then we store the sensation in our brain and it permanently stays there. This is why first impressions are lasting impressions. We do not wipe out the memory of experiences; we only cover them with new memories of later sensations.

By the time each of us has reached adult years, we have developed a lifetime habit of programming our mind to be negative or positive. Two people look at the sunset; one smells the dust and the other sees the dazzling rays of light. One talks about allergies and the other talks about beauty. Jesus looked at Peter and thought about what he could become. Judas looked at Jesus and complained about the wastefulness of precious ointment. Judas talked about how many poor people could be fed with the money from the sale of the ointment. Jesus accepted the extravagance of love symbolized in the pound of ointment. Nothing is more sad than seeing good people spend the first third of their lives programming themselves to be negative and the last two-thirds of life reaping the consequences. And nothing is more wonderful to behold than a self-confident, happy, positive young adult who has programmed faith, hope, and love into a mind that will generate pleasant experiences for all the years to come.

During a management course at the Harvard Business School, a three-day segment was devoted to cybernetics, the comprehensive study of computers. The teacher was, without doubt, one of the finest instructors I have ever known. He was tall, really tall, a commanding presence as he walked around the small horseshoe arena separating the banks of swivel chairs where students listened and watched. At times the class was convulsed in laughter, and moments later, seriously concentrating on some simple analogy that opened a new insight into the operation of a computer. After three days of this kind of teaching and learning, the professor said the time had come for each one of us to sit down for a hands-on operation of a computer.

I walked over to the computer center, sat down at the console of a machine, and began to place data in its brain on the budgetary problems extrapolated out for the next ten years in the college of which I was president. I was concerned about inflation, church support, capital giving, cost of tuition, and other variables that would affect budget figures over the next decade. Each time I punched a figure on the wrong line or in the wrong column, a red light flashed to warn me of my mistake. After forty-five minutes I finally got all of the lines and columns in their proper places as signalled by white letters which flashed on a blue panel with the word "run." I knew the moment of truth had come. I was ready to push the blue panel with the palm of my hand, sit back in the swivel chair, and wait for the computer to perform. I thought it would cycle and re-cycle and flash multi-colored lights as it analyzed the variables related to my budget.

However, when I hit the blue panel with the palm of my hand, and sat back in the swivel chair to watch the performance, nothing happened. Absolutely nothing. There was total and absolute silence. I was just getting ready to kick the machine when I looked up above the regular eye-level to a white panel that was now illuminated. And there in simple numbers and plain English were the answers to the problem I had put into the machine. I could not believe it. There had been no sounds or lights to watch, only the answer. And in one corner of the panel, right at the end of the numbers in the digital display, was the amount of time it took the machine to solve my problem. At Harvard they did not charge out computer time for placing data into the machine, only the amount of time the machine worked to solve the problem. It had taken me forty-five minutes to put my problem into the machine, but it had taken the computer only seven-hundredths of a second to give me an answer.

I slumped back in my chair, feeling inadequate, when the professor came along. "What's the trouble, Les?" he asked. I told him what had happened and how it took forty-five minutes to put my problem into the computer and seven-hundredths of a second for the computer to give me an answer. He became euphoric as he told me about their matching computers on the campuses in Switzerland and in Cambridge and how they bounced the data off of Telestar for instantaneous answers on both sides of the Atlantic. He went on to tell me I could never be a really good college president unless I learned the science of cybernetics and understood fully the operation of the computer, including both its possibilities and its limitations. When he finished I asked if I could pose a question. As he nodded, I went on, "Is it true this computer cost a million dollars?"

He thought for a moment and then replied, "Yes, about a million, two-hundred thousand by the time it was installed."

Then I asked my follow-up question. "Is it also true that all a million-dollar IBM computer can do basically is to take one iota of data and give it a positive electrical impulse and store it, or give it a negative electrical impulse and store it?"

An understanding smile came across his face as he said, "Yes, basically that is right. This computer gives out positive or negative electrical impulses and after that it is a matter of recall, combining, trending, identification, and all the other things the computer can do with the bits of information stored in its memory."

Then I told the professor what I have been writing about in this chapter. The mind is a computer that always has a positive or negative bias. And I find it frightening to think you and I have the power to choose how we will program our minds.

For You or Against You

Most negative people feel they could be positive if they had a different job, a different spouse, lived in the Sun Belt, had a different pastor, or could get cured of their aches and pains. But happiness doesn't come with a new situation. As we go into the new job, move to the Sun Belt, or get a new pastor, we take our same old attitudes into the new situation. A new position soon becomes an unhappy one if we face its inevitable problems with the same old attitudes that have worked against us in the previous job. The divorce that seems necessary and unavoidable is only a threshold to a new kind of hell if our attitudes are working against us. A man with bad attitudes will still be a man with bad attitudes, wherever he lives and whoever his wife is.

Victor Frankl was a twenty-six-year-old Jewish psychiatrist in Vienna, Austria, when he was arrested by Hitler's Gestapo and placed in a concentration camp. Month in and month out, he worked underneath the great smoke stacks that belched out the black carbon monoxide from the incinerators where his father, mother, sister, and wife had been cremated. Each day he hoped for the favor of a line-server who would dip down into the broth a little deeper to come up with a few slivers of carrots or peas in the daily bowl of soup. The soup plus a thick piece of black bread made up the monotonous daily menu. In cold weather he got up an hour earlier than usual to use the burlap and wire he had scrounged to wrap his feet and legs against the crippling cold of an East European winter. His good shoes and warm socks had long since been appropriated by the guards.

When Victor Frankl was finally called for the inquisition, he stood naked in the center of a powerful white light illuminating a small, well defined circle of concrete, while men in shiny boots strode to and fro in the darkened shadows beyond the light. They not only brought him into the room naked, but they shaved his body as a symbolic gesture of his defenselessness. For hours the questions and accusations were shot at him by men with strident voices. They tried to break him down with every accusing lie they could conjure. Already they had taken his precious manuscript, his clothes, his wedding ring, and everything else of material value. But in the midst of this barrage of questions, an idea flashed across the mind of this young Jew, giving him strength and an invincible confidence. He said to himself, in a flash of spiritual insight, "They have taken from me everything I have except the power to choose my own attitudes." We have that same power!

We are living in a day of phobia for physical fitness. Along every highway the joggers jog and the walkers walk. Tennis courts must be reserved and only the most persistent golfers can pay the fees and wait their time to play. Health stores, neighborhood physical health centers, and recreation unlimited is the focus of national attention. Time and energy invested in exercise and recreation are not ill spent. But those who want to be genuinely fulfilled may well shift their primary focus from the physical self to the inner self. Those who invest time and energy in listening to themselves will reap big dividends. If we listen to ourselves, (1) we will soon know what our values and priorities are, (2) we will know whether we are positive or negative people, and (3) we will know whether we have a set of attitudes that are working for us or against us. If you listened to yourself, what would you hear?

Discussion Questions:

1. If you bugged yourself, what topics do you think you'd hear most often?
2. What are the two kinds of basic motivation?
3. What did Isaiah hear when he went into the sanctuary?
4. What are the levels of family conversation as reported in the study at Duke University?
5. Are you basically positive or basically negative?
6. Are your attitudes working for you or against you?

PART II

Affirming the Attitude

We first make our habits, and then our habits make us.

John Dryden

I beseech you therefore, brethren, by the mercies of God, that ye present your bodies a living sacrifice, holy, acceptable unto God, which is your reasonable service. And be not conformed to this world: but be ye transformed by the renewing of your mind, that ye may prove what is that good, and acceptable, and perfect, will of God (Romans 12:1–2).

For this is the will of God, even your sanctification, that ye should abstain from fornication (1 Thessalonians 4:3).

You need never believe that a man can become happy through the unhappiness of another.

Seneca
Epistles to Lucium

6

Renewing Our Minds

It seems a contradiction of fact that good people may have bad attitudes. But it is true. Since some people go to church, pay their bills, maintain their marriages, and do volunteer work, we call them good. But it is also possible these people may not have the habit of happiness. Underneath the external show of goodness, bad attitudes can tarnish all their relationships. Self-righteousness and outward displays of goodness may mask hostility that seethes and burns on the inside. Old-fashioned values, giving to worthy causes, and efforts to avoid the very appearance of evil do not of themselves make people easy to live with. Childhood conditioning by simplistic ideas on being good by doing good has produced some fine, upstanding citizens. And a singular focus on the might and power of orthodoxy can produce some mighty fine people whose highest value is in being right. This kind of religious conditioning can develop Christian adults who would rather fight than be wrong.

Still others whom we rightly perceive as good people sustain their reputations by thinly veiled efforts to deserve their Christian status by what they give of themselves. These good people believe in salvation by grace, but just barely. Although none of these fine folks would support the idea of salvation by works, their Christian service seems to be motivated more by guilt than by love.

I am not trying to discredit the virtues of good people. I am not even trying to discount their motives. I am in favor of orthodoxy and visible displays of goodness. But I am saying it is possible to be perceived as a very fine person and still have bad attitudes that frustrate the habit of happiness.

The second segment of this chapter will be a discussion of St. Paul's suggestions on how we can improve our attitudes by the renewing of our minds. But first, I want to talk about why this renewal is top priority.

The Marvelous Power of Our Words

The renewing of our minds is important because of the power of our attitudes. It is almost impossible to exaggerate this power. We can modify the "power of our attitudes" by adding adjectives such as "incredible" or "super" or "amazing," but even these words cannot overstate this power of the mind God has given us.

Stories about people talking to their plants are common enough but it is now becoming popular to favor plants with music directed specifically to them. Sometime ago I was in the San Joaquin Valley of California for a speaking assignment and saw a large photograph on the front page of the Sacramento newspaper of a grower riding in his helicopter equipped with a microphone, an amplifier, and two giant speakers for singing to his acres of grapes. He insisted the music produced better and sweeter grapes. It is like the idea of contented cows who give more milk when they listen to music during the milking process.

But I want to tell you about the most far-out experiment by reputable scientists I ever heard about. Two researchers in California got the idea they could prove that attitudes make a difference in the germination of seeds. Now you would think that men with Ph.D.'s, wearing white coats, and doing research with government grants would have opted not to act on their idea. Instead they decided to test it.

To prove their point, they used two receptacles somewhat larger than a pie pan, more the size used for gold panning in Alaska. To be sure they had the same quality and quantity of dirt in each one, they put a shingle between them and actually blew the dirt into the pans. Then they counted out twenty-three seeds for the soil in each of the pans followed by the same amount and quality of fertilizer for each. They took the two pans into a greenhouse where they set them in the sun so that both would be subjected to exactly the same temperature and same amount of sunshine during the germination period.

There was only one variable in this experiment. These scientists with Ph.D. degrees, wearing white coats, and using grant money for their study, actually behaved in what seemed to be an irrational fashion. Three times a day they hovered over one pan, and with all of the negativism they could conjure, they attacked those poor, helpless seeds with all kinds of verbal abuse, such as "nothing I ever plant grows . . . . nothing will happen here . . . . if these seeds do sprout, they won't amount to anything . . . . I doubt if they ever come through the soil, and if they do, they will soon die."

Then, three times a day, they turned to the other pan, their personalities now changed. Suddenly they were all smiles. And in pleasant voices they began to say every good and helpful thing they could imagine about the possible germination of the seeds. "I really have a green thumb . . . . everything I ever put in the ground grows . . . . I can hardly wait to see how beautiful these plants are going to be . . . . What we get here is going to be terrific." And with all of the positive emotional expressions they could come up with, these men used their attitudes as reinforcement for the growth and development of the seeds.

Three weeks later, a picture of these two pans appeared in *Time* Magazine. I could not believe what I saw. The pan on the right which had been the object of all their scorn had a few small shoots coming through the ground but could never be considered a full crop. In the pan on the left, which had been the object of their positive reinforcement, there was a full stand of grass that looked strong enough for a person to take hold of and, clutching it, lift the entire pan, dirt and all. The grass must have been eight or nine inches tall and in full flower.

This all happened in the spring of the year while I was preaching a series of sermons during the Lenten season on "All Roads Lead to Jerusalem." One of the messages centered on the experience of Jesus cursing the fig tree that was all leaves and no fruit. And in that sermon, I told the story of the two scientists who had experimented with the power of their attitudes to inhibit or enhance the germination and growth of seeds.

On Tuesday of the next week when I came back into the parsonage at the end of the day, I walked into the family room, our favorite gathering place. On each side of the room were two huge plate glass windows that provided a beautiful vista across the valley to snow-capped Mt. Hood. It was in this room we ate most of our meals, did our telephoning, had family confabs, and did our homework, the children that is. As I walked into the room on this Tuesday, I saw in the plate glass window to the right an old-fashioned Mason jar with a piece of notebook paper around it from a child's notebook, stuck together with Scotch tape, and in a child's handwriting the words, "Yell at." In the other window on the left I saw another Mason jar with a piece of notebook paper around it, held by Scotch tape, and in a child's handwriting the words, "Sweet talk." And I realized my boys were going to test their father's sermon.

Three times every day, those boys went into the family room and yelled at the seeds in one jar and then sweet-talked those in the other. We never had to call them but once in the mornings. They bounded out of bed and headed for the family room for their early morning session with the seeds in the Mason jars. They came straight home from school without delay and immediately went into the family room to yell at and sweet talk the seeds in their jars. They followed the same exercise again at night, just before they went to bed. I have always assumed they got their mother to do the yelling and sweet-talking at noon, but I never could catch her at it.

After nearly three weeks I took those two jars to church with me on a Sunday morning. I arrived early before anyone else was there and placed them beneath the pulpit. In my message that morning I reminded the congregation of the sermon I had preached three weeks before on Jesus cursing the fig tree and the story I had told them of the scientists testing their attitudes on the germination of seeds. The people began to nod indicating they remembered both the sermon and the story. And when I told them the circumstances of my boys deciding to test their father's sermon, there was an immediate response throughout the congregation. I could even hear the choir buzzing behind me.

However, at the appropriate moment, I reached under the pulpit and held up those two Mason jars containing the results of the experiment—the boys yelling at and sweet-talking their seeds. In the right hand jar there were a few blades of grass that had grown up sparsely and scarcely tall enough to be identified. And in the left-hand jar, there was a substantial growth of grass. The sight of these two jars called forth an audible exclamation from the congregation of, "Ah—oh—," accompanied by clearing throats, and such whispered expressions as "Look at that . . . I can't believe it!"

Our oldest son was just going into junior high. He told his science teacher about the experiment and they decided to do a much more sophisticated kind of test using tape recorders with messages every hour on the hour, twenty-four hours a day, for three weeks. At the end of this time, my son took his experiment and the results to the Oregon State Science Fair and won first prize because he had demonstrated the power of attitudes on the germination of seeds.

And the bottom line to this entire story is this. *If attitudes do that to seeds, what do you think they do to human beings?* If attitudes have this power over seeds boys plant in a jar, what do our attitudes do to the minds of our children, or our spouses, or our employees, or our boss?

There are two ways to look at this relationship between attitudes and seeds. We need to be aware of the amazing power of our attitudes in the development of our children and in the other relationships we have in life. But what do we do if we are like the helpless seeds who were yelled at? Are we victims who can never be victors? Do we have responsibility for our attitudes or is our predicament the fault of others? The case I have been making for the habit of happiness is filled with hope. I may be the victim of my childhood but I can become the victor over it.

Seeds do not have a mind of their own. They are governed by an internal mechanism that will respond to proper external stimuli. However, the seed will atrophy, stay dormant, or eventually die if the external stimuli don't provide the right kind of atmosphere for growth. But we are not seeds. We are persons, made in God's own image, possessed of a will for determining how we will react or respond to the external stimuli in our world. This means we can make decisions. We can choose our attitudes and we can decide to be happy in a systematic way, which naturally results in the habit of happiness.

The Analogy of the Tomcat

Before we turn to St. Paul's directives on transforming our minds, I want to illustrate the power of attitudes by giving you the analogy of the tomcat. I have a friend who worked in the laboratory of a great university on the West Coast. He told me about an experiment he and his colleagues did with an old tomcat recruited from the city pound. They kept the cat from food until they were sure he was thoroughly hungry. Then they brought him into the laboratory and began feeding him a popular cat food. The cat was lapping up the food at a rate appropriate to his hunger when the experimenters opened the door of the laboratory and let in a stray dog. There was an immediate emotional response as the cat grew tense, the fur rising on his back. His legs grew tall and his back short as he kept watching the dog out of the corner of his eye, afraid, but unwilling to give up on the food.

All through this experiment the men were watching the cat's insides through a fluoroscope. As he told me in laymen's language, "His insides were purring along like a sewing machine." But as the cat grew more tense and fearful, the digestive system was visibly impaired. Movement of food through the alimentary canal slowed until eventually, according to the experimenter, movement stopped altogether. He said, "The cat kept on eating but nothing was happening to the food on the inside." Then my friend said *"If tension does that to cats, what do you think it does to human beings?"*

It is not only hard to exaggerate the power of our attitudes on others; it is difficult to exaggerate the power of our own attitudes on ourselves. Most of us who suffer from minor aches and pains or even serious ulcer problems will buy help from the drug store for immediate relief from the symptoms. But for permanent healing we might do better to deal with the problem of our own anger or fear which provoked the digestive system to react. There is no doubt that stress, not heart attacks, cancer, or accidents, is the number one killer in America. And stress is closely related to our attitudes.

If we did not have the power within us to change the attitudes that block the habit of happiness, then we would be abandoned in our misery. But the will God has given each of us can be activated in favor of improvement. The habit of happiness is not a dream come true for a few people blessed with a perfect childhood. The habit of happiness is for any person who will make a decision to take responsibility for his unhappiness and do something about changing his attitudes.

If attitudes are powerful and vital, then why, in the name of heaven, do good people have bad attitudes? If attitudes make or break our lives, then why do people ever allow themselves to be torn up with attitudes that are destructive instead of helpful?

Saint Paul, in a single flash of psychological and spiritual insight, put his finger squarely on the reasons. He wrote to his unknown friends in Rome, "I beseech you therefore . . . that ye present your bodies a living sacrifice . . . and be not conformed to this world: but be ye transformed by the renewing of your mind" (Romans 12:1–2). I am always amazed at the way Scripture and studies in human nature confirm each other. In this brief paragraph Paul puts his finger on the three factors that constitute the raw material of attitudes.

Presenting Our Bodies

The first factor in the making of personality is biological. Skin color, size, weight, sex, and degrees of physical attractiveness are all biological factors that we have no control over, with the possible exception of weight control. But these factors, of themselves, do not make our attitudes positive or negative. The way we feel about what we see in the mirror is an important factor in the habit of happiness.

For instance, *how would you feel about yourself if suddenly you were six inches taller than you now are?* For some people, this additional height would be the beginning of a great new life. And for others, it would be pure misery. I know a young lady who has every reason to be proud of herself but is all hung up over the fact that she is more than six feet tall. She slumps in the chair, wears low-heeled shoes, and worries about the height of her boyfriends. She once said to me, "If I go with a boy who is the right height for me, we look like two fugitives from the Celtics basketball team." I once drove her and my wife into Boston's Newberry Street for shopping. As we came off the main artery onto Newberry Street, I saw at the curb what appeared to be the tallest lady I have ever seen in my life. She looked like she was seven feet tall. And to accentuate her height, she wore her hair in an exaggerated beehive. She wore shoes with thick wooden soles that made her look even taller. Without forethought I blurted out, "Oh, my aching back, look at that tall girl!" As I spoke I could just feel this young lady sliding down into the seat of our Buick. And I must say I spent the rest of my time talking about how I like tall girls. I tried to attribute every good quality I could think of to tallness. My friend has every right to hold her head high. She is a fine person. A fine-looking person. But her attitude toward herself keeps her from being a really happy person.

Here is the other side of the same question: *What if you were suddenly six inches shorter than you now are?* What would this do to your personality? For many people, a sudden loss of six inches from their stature would be devastating.

I have a minister friend who will not stand on the platform by the side of a tall man. He makes an issue of waiting until the tall man who announced him has been seated before he will proceed to the podium. For years he had a little stool underneath his pulpit to add another six inches to his height. With a deft move of his toe, he could pull out the stool that just made him feel better about himself because it made him taller. Some said there was more authority in his voice when he stood on his stool. He reminded me of people who drove Volkswagen Beetles, careening in and out through traffic at unnecessary speeds to pass bigger cars and thus prove they could. Can you imagine, for only a moment, what this pastor inflicted on church boards just because he had a hang-up over his height? Most people think of him as hard, inflexible, and sometimes insensitive. These characteristics do not surface because he is bad—only because he cannot reconcile himself to being short.

Here is another question. *If you were not the color you are now, what color would you choose to be?* And, would this make any difference in the way you feel about yourself and others?

Or, *what would happen if you were suddenly fifty pounds heavier than you now are?* It is a myth that fat people are jolly. More often than not, they are dealing unsuccessfully with stress and they alleviate their stress by eating more often than they need to. Any action reduces stress, even if the action is inappropriate. Many nice people are hard on themselves and others because of self-imposed guilt over obesity.

What about physical deformity? Through the years I have been proud of my relationship with college students on the campuses where I have served. But one summer I got a scathing letter. The first few lines were demoralizing. After reading a few paragraphs, I skipped to the end of the letter to see who the writer was. I did not recognize the signer so I phoned the registrar and asked him to bring me the folder of the student whose name was on the letter. There was a picture of each student included in the folders. The registrar walked through my office door some moments later, with the flap of the folder pulled back to the picture of the young lady who had written me the letter. I recognized her at once, and my feelings of defensiveness against her harsh letter turned into understanding.

She was a beautiful young woman who had suffered a diving accident the previous year at summer camp and was paralyzed from her neck down. Although the state paid the bill and the college people, including students, did everything they could to accommodate her physical limitations, she was unable to accept herself after the accident. She lashed out at the people who pushed her wheelchair. She was angry with faculty members and torn up over any and everything that related to her. Her letter to me addressed my ineptness and insensitivity to her needs on campus. My momentary spirit of anger eased into a mellowness as I said to myself, "I really don't know what my attitudes might be if I were forced to cope with the same kinds of physical problems she has."

What would happen if each of us could push a magic button and be the age we would like to be, the height we think is most appropriate, the weight we would enjoy, and possess the physical characteristics we consider to be most beautiful or handsome? Would this make any difference in the kinds of attitudes we have? Without doubt, the results of pushing the magic button would be miraculous. This is why Saint Paul wrote his Corinthian friends, "I beseech you . . . *present your bodies a living sacrifice* to God." People who cannot do this, who cannot accept themselves as they are, invariably have bad attitudes.

Childhood Environment

Another kind of raw material for developing attitudes is our childhood environment, and how we feel about it now. St. Paul said, "I beseech you . . . be not conformed to this world" (Romans 12:1–2). J.B. Phillips translates it "Don't let the world around you squeeze you into its mold." None of us can escape the impact of our early environment. An effective way for opening a small group meeting is to ask everyone present to tell about his home life between the years of ten and twelve. What side of the tracks did you grow up on? What number were you in the family constellation? What was your relationship with Mother and Dad, and their relationship with each other? What kind of plumbing did your house have? How was it heated? Answers to these questions are clues to the way we feel about our lot in childhood.

To illustrate the importance of early environment on the attitudes of adults, I want to tell you about three consecutive Sundays in my own experience. *On the first Sunday I spoke in a small chapel in the ghetto of a great East Coast city.* When the service started two men locked the outside door with a key. When late-arriving people came to the door, both men left their place in the pew to let them in. I watched through the archway as they stepped onto the portico, looked in both directions, came back in, locked the door, and returned to their seats. After the service was over, the pastor said to me, "I will walk with you to your automobile." You might think my car was located a quarter of a mile away from the chapel behind a row of tenement houses. In fact, it was no more than fifty feet from the door of this converted brownstone dwelling.

He said, "Your car is new looking and since it is washed they all know it does not belong down here. You wear a business suit with a white shirt and necktie. All of these things are clear signals that you do not belong. In the next block is the city hospital which includes a methadone center for treatment of drug addicts. These streets are filled with desperate men and women who want help, but would not hesitate a moment to stab you in the back to get enough money for one more fix." Then with firmness he said again, "I will walk with you to your automobile."

Can you imagine for a moment what it might be like to grow up in the ghetto of a great Eastern city where the only means of survival is to join a gang? Any young person who is not a gang member makes himself an easy mark since he has no support system. A child growing up in this setting of the first eighteen years of his life will develop pervasive feelings of helplessness against the waves of social injustice overwhelming his life. He has few defenses. He feels victimized by the political and economic forces that he has no control over. That kind of ghetto environment will make a lifelong impact on a man or woman's attitudes.

On the second Sunday I spoke in a church on the Papago Indian Reservation south of Tucson, Arizona. The congregation consisted of about 150 Indians. They did not smile much, but they could sing. I had seen a special segment on CBS news depicting the depressing poverty, poor health services, inadequate educational opportunities, and job frustrations of these people who lived among the cactus, tumbleweeds, and rattlesnakes of a desert reservation. And now I was seeing them face to face.

At one point in the meeting, the man in charge said, "We are now going to receive an offering for Dr. Parrott." I reached up quickly to take hold of his elbow and whispered, "Please do not do this. My needs are cared for and the offering is not necessary." He pushed my hand aside rather brusquely and continued with the offering. While the ushers were passing the offering plates he sat down by me and said, "If you had refused to allow me to take that offering, these Indians would have thought you did not think their money was important." And so, I publicly accepted $15 from the Papago Indians, returning it to the pastor at lunchtime.

After the service I stayed to talk as long as anyone wanted to, particularly with the young people. They said, "We are the last ones in Tucson to be hired and always the first ones to be fired. People we work for talk about us to each other as though we were not present, like we were some different species who couldn't understand and had no feelings." They told me about their limited education and their fears about leaving the reservation. "Now you tell us," they asked, "how are we to break out of this cocoon and get our part of the good life?"

Can you imagine for a moment what it might be like to live in one of those makeshift houses among the sagebrush and rattlesnakes of the Papago Indian Reservation on an Arizona desert? Would this make any difference in the attitudes that you have as an adult? Would it matter in the way you think about yourself and others?

On the third Sunday I was back on the East Coast in a real First Church of the Middle Class in Charlotte, North Carolina. The church was impressively beautiful. Everything was orderly and well done. The whole operation was a success by the standards of attendance, money, and facilities. Looking out the window of the pastor's study, I saw a luxury automobile whip into the driveway and a family of three children get out with their mother and father. The children were dressed beautifully with coordinated clothes that must have come from a stylish shop. The mother, in a poignant middle class motherly gesture, moistened two fingers and rubbed down the cowlick on the back of the little boy's head. After a quick inspection of the children and a wifely brush of her husband's shoulders, the family was ready to go to church. We do not have to use our imaginations to know that any child growing up in this kind of an upper-middle class setting has material and educational advantages in life totally unknown to the child who grows up in the ghetto or on the Indian reservation.

Maitre D' at the Waldorf

Seattle Pacific University has a tradition I enjoyed when I was a guest there for a lecture series. Following chapel the speaker goes to the student union where he sits at a large round table to talk with students as a follow-up to the chapel talk. After I talked about attitudes the table was swamped with young people filled with questions and comments. We drank coffee and talked for well over an hour, and might not have left then, if it were not for the approaching lunch period.

All the time I was talking with the students I kept my eye on an old gentleman who had joined the group. I rather assumed he was a retired professor, and I also suspected he was waiting with some kind of an academic bomb to drop on me about something I had said. We were about to close the session and he still had not spoken. As a closing gesture I said, "It's nice to have a faculty member at the table, and I wondered, sir, if you have any remarks." His face came aglow as he began telling a story that stopped everybody dead in their tracks. Even the dining room people who had come to set the table stood quietly transfixed as he spoke.

"I am not a professor," he said. "In fact, I have never been to high school. My mother left me in a box on the steps of an orphanage here in Seattle, and I grew up knowing nothing about love and acceptance. When I was just entering my teens, Madame Schumann-Heink, the singer from the Metropolitan Opera, came for a brief concert in our orphanage. Between numbers she announced an offer to pay the way for any boy to go to New York City and become an apprentice for a career as a waiter. When she asked for hands," he said, "I shot mine up immediately, and with one dramatic sweep of her arm, she pointed her finger toward me and I was chosen."

While we all listened, not even budging when the lunch bell rang, the old gentleman continued his story: "I went to New York and was apprenticed as a busboy at the Waldorf-Astoria Hotel. But I hated people. I despised the rich who came to the dining room. And I felt it necessary to compete and, if possible, intimidate the other apprentices. Then one day a young man took me back into the kitchen for a conversation. He told me I was going to ruin my life and my chances for a job and a career if something did not happen that would change my attitudes. He began to tell me about Christ and how faith in him could make all the difference in the way I thought about myself and the way I treated people." I watched as the old man leaned forward resting his hands on the edge of the table, appearing to visualize everything he was telling us. He said, "I listened and thought, and listened some more, and thought again until one day the light was turned on in my mind, and I accepted Christ as Lord of my life."

Then the old man went on with the third segment of his story. "I spent thirty-seven years at the Waldorf-Astoria, and for many of those years, I was the maitre d' dealing with the pressures that are involved with serving a discriminating clientele. Then on retirement, I came back to Seattle, and I have lived here near the University for these last years, going to chapel every time I can. My retirement time is spent visiting people in jail." Then he said something I had never thought of before. "Almost everyone in jail," he said, "has been an abused child, either in an orphanage, a foster home, or in the home of their parents." I realize there surely must be some people in jail who were raised in loving families, but his strong statement makes the point for the importance of childhood environment in determining attitudes in adults.

Not many of us have had the perfect childhood. Broken marriages, alcoholism, drugs, punitive adults, neurotic parents, and moral decline are all too prevalent. If anything, the culture is weighted toward "abnormal childhoods." Even so, there is no reason to let the experiences of childhood persist into the adult years as an ultimate determiner of our attitudes. The world will not squeeze us into its mold unless we allow it. We are no longer children. What happened years ago does not need to dominate us now. Childhood is past history. As adults we are in charge of our lives. If we don't like the attitudes we inherited from childhood then God will help us change them.

The Divine Transformation

St. Paul said, "I beseech you therefore . . . be ye transformed by the renewing of your mind." *The only way I know to change a bad attitude is to change the way we think.* Many good people have bad attitudes in the first place because the strength of the inner self has been watered down and weakened by a pattern of negative responses to life.

After I preached in a large Western church on a Sunday morning, the pastor took me to a fine restaurant for dinner. Because his wife was ill and could not come, we were alone. We had just been served our main entree when he looked up at me and said, "I would like to tell you my story." By the time he had talked for only a moment or two, I began to forget my appetite and soon put down the fork to listen to the story of his transformed life.

He said, "I was actually given away by my father. I well remember the day we went down a dusty country road in an old-fashioned Ford pick-up truck. When he saw a farmer in a field, he honked the horn, and when he got his attention, yelled out of the window, 'How would you like to have a boy?' Apparently the farmer was intrigued because he left his plow and walked over to the fence row where my father waited for him holding onto my hand firmly. The farmer replied as though there had been no gap between the question and the answer, 'Yeah . . . I'd like to have a boy if he can work.' I well remember the feeling I had when my father turned toward me and without saying a word put his hands underneath my arm pits and, in a matter of seconds, lifted me over the fence and stood me down on the other side facing the farmer as I screamed and stomped out of sheer fright. When I turned around to look, my father was already on his way back toward the pick-up truck, never looking back at me for a wave or a good-bye. The mental picture I have of him disappearing down the road in a cloud of dust is something I can never forget.

"The farmer only kept me a short while because I was small and not able to work as hard as he wanted me to work. He put me in an orphanage. And inside, things went from bad to worse. I was the smallest of the boys in my age group, and the others all picked on me. Life was miserable. And I responded with anger, acting out my hostility with verbal and physical abuse. The couple in charge of the orphanage considered me a trouble maker. And the more I disrupted things at the orphanage the harder they were on me.

"One day somebody came in and said a Sunday school bus was coming to the orphanage the next Sunday morning, and anybody who wanted to go could go. They also made it plain that nobody needed to go if they did not want to. Since I would do anything to get away from that place, I was waiting the next Sunday morning with my face scrubbed when the bus pulled up in front of the orphanage and I got in. I had no idea where it was going. I knew nothing about the church. That really didn't matter to me. I just wanted to get out of the orphanage.

"At the church I found people like I had never seen before. I did not know people like this existed who were kind, who spoke directly to you and waited for an answer as though what you were going to say mattered to them. After the service was over, someone took me home with their family for a meal like I had never seen before in all my life. There were happy children playing in the house and later outside on the lawn. The father and mother spoke kindly to each other and to the children. It was one of the first times I can remember when I had my fill of really good food."

The months became years as this young man continued his life in the orphanage on weekdays and in the church on Sunday. "Finally," he said, "I was about to enter my last year in high school when the people in the church began to talk to me about going to college. I told them this was impossible because no one in our family had ever gone to college. I had never seen a college, and I was sure I would not have enough money to enroll. They said they would provide the money and they would help me find the college where I could get the best education for me." My friend went on to tell me how he enrolled in college and later felt a call into the ministry of the denomination whose local congregation had been kind to him. He married a fine young lady, and finally was given a pastoral assignment.

"But," he said "I found that I could not get on with any of the strong members in the church. Every time a board member or a woman with a strong voice said something the least bit harsh toward me, I had recurring visions of the monitors at the orphanage and officials who had bedeviled my life. I did the only thing I knew to do, which was to strike back hard and fast, just as I did in the sleeping quarters of the orphanage. I had learned to strike back hard at bullies who looked or acted in a threatening way. If my blow was strong enough and quick enough, I learned the bully would tend to leave me alone. But now in the church, I was only alienating the people I was trying to serve.

"Finally," he said, "I went to the altar of our church on a weekday when no one else was in the building. Defeated, demoralized, and facing sure defeat in my responsibilities as a pastor, I confessed my own predicament to God and told him I was not willing to go on any longer living like this. I wanted to put behind me all that had ever happened and start a whole new life with attitudes that would help me. I don't know what happened to me that day, only that my entire life changed. And from then on, I worked on the assumption that God could help me to live in the present and not be defeated by all of the things that had happened to me in the past. I had experienced a hard life in the orphanage, but I had also experienced a good life among compassionate people in the church. My opportunity was not behind me, but before me. And from that day on, my ministry took on an entirely new level of effectiveness."

Since the day this minister told me his story, I have watched his life with great interest. After all these years, he is still pastor of the same congregation. The last I heard, there was talk about bulldozing his church and building a larger sanctuary to hold the crowds that come to hear him preach.

It is not possible to change the biological factor in our lives. If we are born to be short, we will be short. If we tend to be fat, we will probably keep on being fat in spite of our occasional flurries of dieting. If we are uncoordinated, we will continue being uncoordinated. If we are black, we will always be black. And if we are Indian, we will always be Indian. The biological factors in our physical being are set. *Also, our early childhood environment cannot be changed.* Even God, himself, will not turn back the calendar. What was done in childhood is done. It is over and past. *But there is one thing that can be changed. Our minds can be transformed.* God can help us change the way we think about the past and about ourselves. God can help us transform our minds.

Discussion Questions:

1. Do you really believe attitudes affect plants, or is the idea only imaginary?

2. How do we present our bodies as living sacrifices to God?

3. What things happened in your childhood that still make a difference in your attitudes?

4. In what ways can our minds be transformed?

Blessed is the man that walketh not in the counsel of the ungodly, nor standeth in the way of sinners, nor sitteth in the seat of the scornful. But his delight is in the law of the Lord; and in his law doth he meditate day and night. And he shall be like a tree planted by the rivers of water, that bringeth forth his fruit in his season; his leaf also shall not wither; and whatsoever he doeth shall prosper. The ungodly are not so: but are like the chaff which the wind driveth away. Therefore the ungodly shall not stand in the judgment, nor sinners in the congregation of the righteous. For the Lord knoweth the way of the righteous: but the way of the ungodly shall perish (Psalm 1).

When I was a child, I spake as a child, I understood as a child, I thought as a child: but when I became a man, I put away childish things (1 Corinthians 13:11).

Wherefore seeing we also are compassed about with so great a cloud of witnesses, let us lay aside every weight, and the sin which doth so easily beset us, and let us run with patience the race that is set before us (Hebrews 12:1).

I never knew a man to overcome a bad habit gradually.

John R. Mott

7

How to Change a Negative Attitude

It would be wonderful if everyone were born with Babe Ruth's optimism. Winners keep on winning and losers keep on losing. But it need not be that way. The negative attitude is amenable to change. A negative person can become positive. Let me try to shed light on this process through several different windows of understanding.

When I first saw how much the mind works like a computer, the thought gave me a new breath of understanding. Programmers are well paid people who design what goes into the memory bank of a computer. Once the program is in operation it is fine tuned to remove the "bugs," and then the program runs indefinitely performing what it was programmed to do.

The most incredible computer the world knows anything about is the human brain. I once heard a scientist say that a man-made computer with the capacity to do all the things the human brain does would need a building as large as the Empire State Building to house it and half of all the power turned out by Niagara Falls to run it. And it would still be doubtful if the man-made computer could do all the things that are done by the human brain. The micro chip has scaled down the size of the building needed for the man-made computer that could compete with the brain and has reduced the need for half the energy from Niagara Falls to operate it. But high technology has not changed the awesome fact that the human neural system operates with efficiency that makes the telephone networks look cumbersome and prone to error.

There are several differences between a man-made computer and the human brain.

(1) To begin with, the human brain never rests. Even while we sleep the brain continues to express our subliminal wishes through dreams and react to our overpowering and shattering fears through nightmares.

(2) The human computer is totally portable.

(3) This diminutive package of about two pounds is us. The brain cannot be separated from the body. It is possible for a person to be brain dead while the heart still beats, but life has lost its meaning.

(4) The human computer has the capacity to store feelings while the man-made computer is purely mechanical. In the human computer emotions usually take precedence over pure statistical information. Although we may not remember someone's name we usually remember how we felt about him. We may dislike the person and not really know why. "It's just a feeling I have."

(5) The human computer has the capacity to distort anything in its memory bank. For instance, the human brain, like the man-made computer, has the capacity for instant recall. We can reach back a year, or ten years, or seventy-five years if we are fortunate enough to live that long and recall in living color the events that have meaning to us. However, as the pictures move across the screen of our memory we have the capacity to stop the reel and enlarge or diminish any frame to suit our purposes. Or, under acute pain, we can block out a picture from our consciousness and send it to the subterranean filing system of the mind where it is kept alive but out of sight.

(6) The human computer can be reprogrammed while it

continues to run. The amount of "down time" in a mainframe computer operation is one of the hi-tech inconveniences. Have you ever called a major airline for a reservation and been asked to call back because the computer was down? This doesn't happen with the thought patterns of the human brain. It can be adjusted, reprogrammed, or made extinct while the mind continues to do its work.

(7) The human computer is highly subjective while the man-made computer is entirely deterministic; what goes in is what comes out. In the human computer there are ameliorating elements that give meaning to the flow of information. A mechanical computer has no capacity for dealing with intangibles such as love, hate, compassion, sensitivity, insensitivity, loyalty, deviousness, commitment, or self-centeredness. However, these human characteristics can change what goes into the human computer and make it come out in a more positive or negative way than it was received.

The habit of happiness is the continuing affirmation of life. This affirmation takes place in the mind where our thought patterns are always subject to review and correction. The change from a negative to a positive person is not an overnight wonder like a shot of penicillin that quickly destroys the virus and lets the body heal itself. It is a self-educating process, more like a pilgrimage than a hospital experience. It is learning by doing; it is not being a passive patient in an operating room waiting for specialists to do for us what we don't know how to do for ourselves.

Even while he was here on earth, the Great Physician was more a teacher than a surgeon. His miracles were moments of divine intervention in a process of self-help that preceded and followed the event. The 5,000 were not fed until a little boy gave all he had and the disbelieving disciples changed their negative attitudes and began organizing the people into manageable groups for serving. No one knows what happened to the twelve baskets of leftovers but it certainly was not part of a continuous miracle that made working for their daily food no longer necessary. The blind man waited patiently for Jesus to pass by, believing there was help for his sightless eyes. Still blind, he was sent by Jesus to the pool with instructions to wash off the spittle and the clay. He later stood up to the hostile scribes and Pharisees who found no joy in his healing.

It takes both the human and the divine for the mind to be reprogrammed from negative to positive. The problem is not all yours. God will help you. But the responsibility is not all his because he expects your involvement in the process.

The reprogramming of a negative mind is a process, but there are great moments of insight and understanding that help us make quantum leaps ahead.

All of us who are interested in developing the habit of happiness and improving the positive quality of our attitudes will find help in three areas of human flexibility: (1) An improved self-respect can be programmed into our minds by changing the way we think about ourselves. (2) Maturity can be increased by monitoring our level of self-centeredness, our tendency to use abusive language, and our dependence on conditioned religion. (3) The will is a phenomenal power in affirming life through our attitudes.

How Do You Picture Yourself?

The first step in altering a negative mindset is to change the way we feel about ourselves. Anything that improves the mental fix we have on ourselves brings us nearer to the habit of happiness. Some years ago a plastic surgeon in New York observed that some patients, who had fairly minor face surgery, such as the removal of a mole, immediately experienced an unusual positive change in their attitudes and sense of self-worth. But, he observed that other people, who underwent significant surgery, such as a facelift or the change of a nose line, came out of the operation with little attitudinal improvement. They remained sunken in negative feelings and attitudes, and ways of doing things, which had already overshadowed their lives before surgery. The doctor finally set aside his tools as a plastic surgeon and picked up those of a social scientist to find an answer to this dis-crepancy. Dr. Maltz's full answer is found in his best-selling book of a generation ago called *Psycho-Cybernetics*. He con-cluded that anything that changes the way we see ourselves will change our personality.

One agent of change may be cosmetic surgery. There are things that help us alter the way we feel about ourselves. A five-year-old who passes his sixth birthday and enters the first grade will often change his personality. And men and women who pass into their fourth decade often begin to see them-selves in a new way. Time changes their attitudes. Youth is gone and middle age is at hand. Weight loss or gain can change the way we think about ourselves, and therefore, change our personalities. A new job with higher status will often change the feelings we have about ourselves while the loss of a job that leaves us with a sense of failure may reverse our positive feelings. Maybe this is why Jesus found the expression "born again" as the most descriptive idea he could use in explaining forgiveness to Nicodemus. When our load of guilt is gone, we begin to think differently about ourselves. Therefore, a basic step toward the habit of happiness is to decide what we can do about ourselves to improve our self-respect.

Some years ago, Dr. Missildine, who was head of the School of Psychiatric Training at Ohio State University, set up a clinic in downtown Columbus for disturbed children. He found that the tools of the psychoanalytic approach, which called for long periods of therapy, were slow, expen-sive, sometimes frustrating, and not always effective. He be-gan an earnest search for a better way of dealing with the problems of children, which he discussed in his helpful book, *Your Inner Child of the Past*.

Dr. Missildine says that each of us is born with two fears, loud noises and the loss of support, or falling. Almost every-thing else in our response system is learned. He says that we learn from a small group usually consisting of no more than four or five persons including mother, father, brother or sis-ter, a close relative, neighbor, or teacher. These important people give meaning to our lives by telling us who we really are. The way they listen to or ignore us, or the way they slap us or love us, or tell us to shut up, or give us a worthy answer, are all small pieces of the picture puzzle being shaped, piece by piece, in our minds. In a multitude of ways when we are children the important adults in our lives begin to tell us who we are. By the time we have reached our early teens, Dr. Missildine says we have learned very well that we are beautiful or ugly, smart or dumb, fast or slow, that we like spinach or we don't, can spell or cannot, hate arithmetic or love it. Sometime between the years of thirteen and fifteen this mental picture of ourselves becomes complete.

Then Dr. Missildine asks, "What happens to this inner picture of ourselves as we change from being a child to becoming an adult?" Does one's picture of himself as a child fade away? Does it suddenly dissolve? Is it forgotten?

The answer to all these questions is, "No!"

In fact, this picture of ourselves as children is the same picture most of us keep in our minds for the rest of our lives. The inner child of the past is our point of reference for all our adult attitudes. Like the layers of an onion, we begin to wrap that inner child of the past with the trappings of adulthood. There is the layer of formal education, the layer of family responsibility, and layers of career expectations, social status, and many more. But down below all the layers of adult sophistication is the self-concept hidden deep inside, at the core of life. We may be six feet tall, sitting behind an important desk, or have the adult figure of a fashion model, but down in our psyche we are dominated by the attitudes that developed out of the picture we have of ourselves as children.

There is every reason for a small child to feel inferior and inadequate. We grow up subject to the strength and authority of big people. We must look up at the undersides of tables and see adults like huge giants. If we start to please ourselves by resisting the will of one of these adults, we are immediately snatched up and set down in another place, struck, yelled at, or spanked. All through childhood we are "disciplined" by adults who "know best."

During the teen years, we feel strong urges to be our own person, free from the authority of the adults who have dominated our lives. However, we have neither the external resources nor the internal strength to effect this freedom. The teen years are not happy-go-lucky years. They are more likely to be years of inner conflict, wide swings in emotional responses, and uncertainty about big decisions like education, career, sex, and life values. And, if we are influenced by a negative, harsh, insensitive adult during these important years, the fears of childhood will turn into the active rebellion of the teen years. The negative adult is likely to be the adult who hangs on to the negative picture given him in childhood.

What can a negative person do? Obviously, there is no way to go back and start life over with a more positive set of adults. We can keep on being negative and thereby make ourselves and everyone around us miserable. Or, we can work at the process of changing the picture of ourselves. How can we improve or change the image we have of ourselves?

We may decide the original picture taken years ago is outdated and replace it with an updated version. People who called us dull or ugly may have been partially correct. If we were slow learning to walk or talk we may have prompted some unknowing adult to really believe we were dumb. Childhood features like big ears or flat noses can create a caricature in people's minds and they pin us with a cruel nickname like frog or snooze. Late bloomers and ugly ducklings can grow up with inaccurate mental pictures of themselves. Education, life experiences, and our own will to learn may have changed an earlier picture we had of ourselves. We may have inherited a body no Grecian god would claim and a face that is not photogenic, but we may also have developed social graces, used clothes to our advantage, and observed that our friends enjoy our company. We may observe we are now more at ease with people than we were when adults decided we were shy. Reassessing what we are like now against what our memory says we were in earlier years may be a helpful step in changing our mental image.

We may decide the original self-photo, which we have

carried with us all these years, was blemished and inaccurate when it was taken. As Dr. Missildine suggests, our original mental picture of ourselves is the composite work of all the people whose opinions made a difference in the way we saw ourselves. But they may have been wrong. We may have seen ourselves as unworthy and unlovable because we were ignored, slapped around, or punished severely.

Adults may have treated us badly for several reasons: (1) Surrogate parents may not have had the sense of parental pride and loving care often associated with real parents. (2) In some homes and institutions there may not have been enough love to go around. (3) Some parents are so completely wrapped up in their own neurotic needs they have no love to spare. (4) Some parents are ignorant of the psychological needs of children and ill advised on how to discipline them. Therefore the child is either ignored or punished in terms that meet the frustrated needs of the adult and not the child. (5) The blending of two families in a second marriage can send mixed signals to children as to their self-worth.

Parents and other significant adults do make mistakes. They do send wrong signals, which blemish children's pictures of themselves. If our self-picture is inaccurate we have the right and the responsibility to change it in harmony with present reality.

Finally, it is possible to develop a new picture of ourselves in terms of what we can become. How we help other people change their mental image through encouragement has been explained in many places. But I am concerned about how we may improve our self-image when we have no one to help us. The writer of Hebrews said, "Faith is *the substance* of things hoped for, *the evidence* of things not seen" (Hebrews 11:1). For years I have used a psychologist's paraphrase of this verse which has helped me to develop achieving faith when I really had none: "Faith (which is a positive attitude) is the substance (mental picture) of things hoped for, the evidence (behaving as though the mental picture were already developing) of things unseen." A positive attitude begins with a mental picture we believe will become true if we have enough confidence to start acting like we think it will. Professional golfers visualize each shot before they make it. Builders have a mental picture of a finished structure before they begin construction. And every person who has the capacity to visualize himself has the potential to change his mental image.

To get the process in motion follow this simple plan: (1) Divide a sheet of paper into three columns. (2) In column one, list the characteristics you see in yourself. (3) In column two, list the characteristics you would like to develop. (4) And in column three, write out the specific things you can do to help develop these characteristics. Set dates for monitoring your progress. Some people find it helpful to keep a daily log. To change ourselves we must decide specifically what we want to change and how we are going about it. But during this entire process never lose sight of the person you plan to become.

From Here to Maturity

A wise old man once wrote a letter to some friends who were living in a Roman outpost designated as a frontier city. Recruits from the Roman army were given special bonuses for settling in the city of Corinth. These inducements must have been like the free land offered American citizens when the West was first settled under the Homestead Act. Most people moved to Corinth to get away from the past, to make a quick fortune, or to live free from the ancient moral codes. Sex, violence, and materialism were the major topics of conversation on the streets of Corinth. The only basis for any deal was self-interest. "Love" was contracted on the basis of pay for services rendered, like any other commodity. Bizarre religious faith represented itself in temple prostitutes and strange tongues. It was every man for himself in the Hollywood of its day.

But in the midst of this secular city, there was a band of humble Christians trying to live a positive life in a negative environment. Paul wrote a letter to these Christians in

Corinth, a letter that included three observations on changing a negative way of life. He said, "When I was a child, *I spake* as a child, *I understood* as a child, *I thought* as a child: but when I became a man, *I put away childish things*" (1 Corinthians 13:11).

Nothing is sadder than adults trying to cope with the challenges of home and family while depending on a set of emotions and patterns of thinking that crystallized during their early teens. Life is a continuing process of growth and development. The level of our maturity at fifteen years of age will not be adequate at thirty or forty. Negativism is not a synonym for immaturity. But negative people have immature ways. Abiding love is the ultimate expression of maturity. It is impossible to love others as we love ourselves and be immature in our relationships. Also, it is impossible to love God and not affirm life. In this passage Paul gives guidance to Christians who want to improve the level of their maturity.

Thinking Like a Child

"When I was a child . . . I thought as a child: but when I became a man, I put away childish things" (1 Corinthians 13:11).

When a baby is conceived, it lives for nine months in the womb, protected from injury, fully dependent on the life of its mother. Growth and development of the fetus is at the expense of the mother. The mother provides the blood, minerals, protein, and all else the baby needs. Even when the child is born, it is not shoved out into a cruel, cold world as we sometimes say. The baby is more often delivered into the center of its own private world. Couples sometimes rebuild their houses, or at least remodel a room to receive their baby. Money, which could have been used for other family needs, is often spent on expensive baby equipment and accouterments to make the child as beautiful and happy as possible. Schedules are revamped and priorities adjusted to meet every need of the baby.

We went through some shocking adjustments when our first son was born after years of waiting. Everything changed, or almost everything. I found notes pinned to the front door warning me against knocking, slamming the door, shuffling my feet, or doing anything else that would disturb the baby. When he awakened in the middle of the night and cried, we had a contest to see who could get to his side first. After his room was papered with elves, and lacy white cottage curtains were hung, we moved the baby's bassinet to the middle of the room. He and his room were the center of our world. We no longer stayed out late at night, or picked up at a moment's notice to go join friends who were eating out. We looked after the baby and saw that his needs were fully met.

I well remember the Sunday morning we took him to church for the first time. I was dressed in my black suit and striped tie, with my Bible under my arm, ready to preach the morning sermon. My wife was holding the baby as we moved from the parlor into the hallway leading to the front door. Suddenly I stopped her. It just did not seem right for her to be carrying the child. Like a good father, I picked him up in my arms and started to rest him on my shoulder. But as I moved him about, he had a very uncomfortable feeling down in his mid-section that he relieved by spitting sour milk all over my black suit, across my tie and shirt, and all over my Bible. With no time to change, I cleaned up myself the best I could, sprayed on some perfume, and went on to church. The baby was not even aware and, therefore, had no concern for what he had done to me. The baby's only concern was for himself. He wanted relief from his own pain; and what happened to me was my business. Every baby is born completely self-centered. During his first days he does not even differentiate the world around him from himself. His mother is an extension of himself. From this ultimate self-centered start, the baby begins the long journey toward maturity. The lifelong task is to move from self to others.

When the child is about two years of age we say it's time for him to begin learning how to bear minor frustrations. Babies are to be babied for two years, and then we begin the process of letting them know there are other people in the world they must reckon with. Toys must be shared. Other people's rights must not be ignored. Education is the lifelong process of learning to live with everybody else.

I once asked a psychiatrist for his definition of original sin. He responded by describing a small child's self-centeredness and the process of moving from self to a broader concern for others. But any time an adult reverts to infantile behavior and childish self-centeredness that excludes others, he has, according to this psychiatrist, reverted to original sin. "When I was a child . . . I thought as a child: but when I became a man, I put away childish things" (1 Corinthians 13:11).

Talking Like a Child

Children can devastate others with their tongues. They can say the most demeaning things to each other and to adults. I knew a small boy once who knew how to devastate his young mother completely. He was small, but not too small to realize she was fighting a losing battle on weight control. In his moments of ultimate exasperation he called her "fatty." With one word well spoken, he destroyed her self-confidence, hit her most vulnerable nerve, and left her defenseless. And the child did all this damage with just one word. What a commentary on the ability of a child to speak like a child!

Jesus understood the way children talked. Tucked away in the Gospel record is a parable so small it could be missed. He asked the question, "What is this generation like?" (see Matthew 11:16). Jesus said they were like children in the marketplace. One group sits down on one side of the street and another on the opposite side while they make up little rhymes to taunt one another. One group sings, "We have harped and you have not danced," and the other children cry back in chorus, "But we have wept and you have not mourned." One commentator suggests that in the original Aramaic language this taunting exchange was a little rhyme children used to aggravate each other.

Abusive tongues may be accepted as normal among children, but the conversations of mature adults are nonviolent and unabusive. The man who says, "So and so is a nice person, *but* . . ." is really saying, "When I think about him, I feel very inadequate; so spare me a few moments to pull him down to my size, and then we will go on with this conversation." There is no other explanation for backbiting and negativism except our own insecure feelings of inferiority and inadequacy.

None of us can go back and relive the experiences of our childhood. If our home environment helped make us a negative adult, we can only accept this for what it is and begin to learn how to put away childish talking and replace it with mature, adult conversation based on a willingness to let people be like they are instead of the way we wish they were. Paul said, "When I was a child, I spoke as a child . . . but when I became a man, I put away childish things" (1 Corinthians 13:11).

Conditioned Learning

Small children do not learn by reasoning. They learn by conditioning. The classical form of conditioning has been explained in the writings of B. F. Skinner as positive reinforcement. If a baby learns that screaming will bring mother on the run, then he will scream. But the sad part of the story is that he will continue to scream in later years after the effectiveness of the small child's screaming technique has worn off. If a little girl learns that being winsome is an effective way to get what she wants from father, in competition with her brothers, then she will be winsome. But this may also raise unrealistic expectations among the men in her adult life who do not give in to her winsome ways except to take advantage of her.

A mother warns her two-year-old not to wander out into the street. Her warning includes references to several concepts the small child does not understand such as "dangerous" and "fast" automobiles, "heavy" trucks, "terrible" wrecks, and "awful" hospitals. However, when boredom sets in while playing near the house, the child who does not understand the abstractions in mother's severe warning will wander out toward the street, having no twinge of conscience for disobeying, and for the moment, no fear of the consequences. Then the mother comes running through the screen door letting it bang in a terrifying clap behind her. Scooping up the child in her protective arms she lectures him loudly and sternly. Then she conditions his reflexes through a tearful spanking.

The preschooler keeps away from the street and plays again up toward the safer area near the house. After this process of the loud lecture and the spanking have been repeated two or three times, the child will, according to his I.Q., begin to associate an unpleasant experience with something that happens to him when he plays close to the street. He still does not understand his mother's logic and fears, which relate to him the speed, frequency, and weight of automobiles and trucks on his street. But he learns to stay away from the danger area because his mother has conditioned him to keep away from the street to avoid a spanking.

Conditioned learning in small children is expected, but it is deplorable in adults. The immature side of a negative personality will give way to the positive outlook of maturity in the person who decides to give up childish understanding. Paul said, "When I was a child . . . I understood as a child . . . but when I became a man, I put away childish things" (1 Corinthians 13:11).

Faith is believing, hope is anticipating, and love is accepting. Faith believes in God, self, and others. Hope anticipates a better future. And love accepts the people in our little personal world just as they are. The mature adult affirms life with these three great values Paul used in closing his admonition: "And now abideth faith, hope, charity, these three; but the greatest of these is charity" (1 Corinthians 13:13). In the context of reaching for maturity, faith and hope are the laser beams that reach out to the farthest stars in our firmament. But love is the sunlight that encompasses our universe.

Erotic love between a man and a woman, the love among friends, and family love are three different kinds of love kept alive only in reciprocal relationships. It takes two people to make love, to maintain a friendship, or form a family unit. The kind of love in these relationships demands giving and receiving, reaching out and accepting back. But there is another kind of love, an unbeatable good will, that does not depend upon the response of another person. This is unconditional love, the kind Christ had on the cross. He gave himself and they spat in his face, but he kept on giving. This kind of love in men and women comes from an inner resource that provides the power to have accepting feelings toward other people, whether or not they return our love. This is the ultimate level of Christian maturity.

Both Mahatma Gandhi and Martin Luther King were bitter young men who were dominated by negative attitudes until they learned the meaning of a love not dependent on reciprocity. The negativism of Gandhi in India and Africa and King in the United States faded into unbeatable campaigns for social justice when each in his own turn learned that the hate and violence of their enemies did not need to condition their responses. Love is nonviolent; it never abuses.

Discussion Questions:

1. In what ways is a computer like our minds?

2. How do we develop our inner child of the past?

3. In what ways can the mental picture we hold of ourselves be wrong?

4. What are the three ways of a child which maturity can put away?

5. Which is the most harmful, verbal abuse or physical abuse?

PART III

Facing Ourselves

Happiness is neither virtue nor pleasure, but simply growth. We are happy when we are growing.

J. B. Yeats

Do ye think that the scripture saith in vain, The spirit that dwelleth in us lusteth to envy? But he giveth more grace. Wherefore he saith, God resisteth the proud, but giveth grace unto the humble. Submit yourselves therefore to God. Resist the devil, and he will flee from you. Draw nigh to God, and he will draw nigh to you. Cleanse your hands, ye sinners; and purify your hearts, ye doubleminded. Be afflicted, and mourn, and weep: let your laughter be turned to mourning, and your joy to heaviness. Humble yourselves in the sight of the Lord, and he shall lift you up. Speak not evil one of another, brethren. He that speaketh evil of his brother, and judgeth his brother, speaketh evil of the law, and judgeth the law: but if thou judge the law, thou art not a doer of the law, but a judge. There is one lawgiver, who is able to save and to destroy: who art thou that judgest another? (James 4:5–12).

Human felicity is produced not so much by great pieces of good fortune that seldom happen, as by little advantages that occur every day.

Benjamin Franklin
Autobiography

130

8

How Attitudes Can Make
or Break Our Lives:
An Explanation

It is no accident that some people live radiant, happy, productive lives while others, who go to the same church, hear the same sermons, and sing out of the same hymnbook, live lives that are beaten down, defeated, and anxiety-ridden.

It is no accident that some people seem to take all life hands them in stride, rising above disappointments and heartaches in a continuing attitude of happiness while others who have had the same educational advantages, lived in the same suburbs, and had comparable incomes, are dominated by feelings of anger, jealousy, boredom, and loss of enthusiasm.

It is no accident that some people may be transferred to any community, assigned any job, and be faced with any series of obstacles when suddenly, on their arrival, factors beyond their control in the situation begin working to their advantage. Their own attitudes plus the attitudes of the people with whom they work start accruing in their favor.

At the same time, other people go through life plagued by dead-end job assignments, bad patterns in decision making, and a totally inept approach to living which brings their world tumbling in about them and sends all of their friends and associates, who could be of help, into the far country of looking on and waiting to see what is going to happen next.

There are reasons for these discrepancies in good and bad "luck," positive providential happenings, and the ability or lack of ability to deal with the good and bad.

The Laws of God in the Physical Universe

Visualize, for a moment, the chalkboard in a classroom with perpendicular lines on it representing the laws God has built into the universe. Any person who expects to live out his or her normal life span with a reasonable degree of good health and not be accident prone must learn how to live in harmony with the laws these lines represent. It does not matter if we know about the laws God built into the universe or not. Ignorance of the rules affords no exemption. And there is no place in the physical systems of this world for thoughtlessness or forgetfulness. Those who break God's laws are the object of their own punishment. These are not arbitrary laws made by a capricious God. They are the laws that hold the world together. For the sake of our own enlightened self-interest we live in harmony with these laws in the physical universe. If we choose to go against these laws we face the wrath of God which is the ill wind of consequences that blows in the face of any and all who set their will against God.

An illustration of this concept of the laws of God that govern the universe is the silly man who says he does not believe in the law of gravity. Just because he is an existentialist and a free thinker, no exception is made in his case if he jumps off a tall building. The law of gravity is not broken. He is. There is no favored status when gravity self-destructs. The physical laws of the universe are never intimidated. The driver who goes to sleep at the wheel is killed when he strikes the bridge at high speed (whether he is a good man or a bad man) because the laws that hold this world together do not have rewards and punishments, only consequences.

In May of 1961 John Kennedy announced a decision to put a man on the moon by 1970. When I heard his announcement on national television, I could not have been more shocked if he had proclaimed a cure for cancer. People were still reading comic books about trips into outer space. Saturday morning cartoons still held children spell-bound with characters who traveled on space ships between planets. But no one, at least not many, took the possibility of travel in outer space seriously until the president put the moon trip on the national agenda.

But we did it. Or, at least, it was done. And we, as a nation, achieved the goal of a successful trip to the moon because our government and our scientists were willing to pay the price for research on the laws that govern outer space and for the development of hardware and programs based on their knowledge of these laws. Our scientists did not invent the laws that govern outer space. They discovered them and then worked at the task of learning how to live in harmony with those laws.

Our scientists knew they would never put a man on the moon safely and bring him back again just because they were good Americans who could sing "The Star-Spangled Banner" and recite the Pledge of Allegiance to the American flag. Goodness was not the issue, knowledge was. This trip to the moon and back was accomplished because our people were willing to invest enough time, money, and brainpower to master the necessary information about the laws of this universe that relate to outer space.

Today you can go into any university library in the world and find shelves of doctoral dissertations on these laws of God that govern the universe. Sometime ago I heard a scientist say that 97 percent of all the world's greatest scientists who have ever lived are alive right now. And, he said, these people have learned more about the laws of the universe in the last fifteen years than has been known in the last fifty years. And he further said they have learned more in the last fifty years than has been known about these laws since the dawn of creation.

The Laws of God in Human Nature

And now, keep this concept in mind—the laws that govern the physical universe—while we turn to another side of the imaginary chalkboard to draw some perpendicular lines that represent the laws of God in human nature. We know less about the laws of God in human nature than we do the laws of the universe. You cannot go into every great university in the world and find shelves of Ph.D. dissertations written about these laws, but that does not make them any less true. When Jesus said, "Let us make man in our own image," he was not talking about ears and eyes and nose. God is a spirit. The image of God is in the inner spirit of man. And when that inner spirit is out of sync with the laws of God in man's nature and alienated from God by willful separation, the results are a bedeviled life of "bad luck."

And again, as with the laws governing the physical universe, ignorance of these laws in human nature is no excuse. These laws in the psyche affect our lives whether or not we understand them or whether or not we make any effort to live in harmony with them. Either we will live in step with the laws of God in human nature or we will pay enormous penalties in the lack of personal satisfaction, frustrated careers, poor mental and physical health, broken relationships even with the people we need most, and the possibility of an empty, pointless life.

People who go against these laws of God in human nature have lines in their faces beyond their years. They suffer from psychosomatic illnesses, wall to wall. When some people reach a certain age, they would do well to put a doctor on a retainer and send him a check once a month for the rest of their lives. They are going to be visiting a variety of physicians with increasing regularity as they move inexorably toward physical and emotional exhaustion and the human breakdown that follows. Many of their symptoms, such as vague aches and pains, unexplainable rashes, certain respiratory difficulties, and even some lower back problems, are often rooted in the torn-up psyche. Emotional disarray is the black soil of the mind which sprouts the nebulous pains that grow to dominate our lives.

A person trying to cope with the throbbing problems of a strained marriage relationship often thinks the difficulty rests mainly with the spouse. Search for help usually takes its departure from that point on the responsibility compass, which says I should look for the source of my problems in you. In the old days marriage counselors tried to determine who was wrong. However, more current social scientists know there is a delicate balance that sustains every relationship; and this relationship can be upset by any kind of change that threatens the emotional or attitudinal equilibrium of the persons involved. It's not who's wrong, but what's wrong that counts. Apathy, boredom, the tendency to project the causes of our problems on others, and almost every other symptomatic problem in the fulfillment of our lives can be traced to a breakdown in our personal relationship with the laws of God governing human nature.

Unfortunately, when a person suffering with psychosomatic illness goes to a doctor, the physician knows he does not have a scalpel, a pill, or a capsule to get at the root of the problem. Therefore, the doctor takes the only practical option open to him; he deals with the symptom. And he also knows that the symptom masking the real problem will go underground after treatment only to come back again in the same or another form. Some people are addicted to going from one doctor to another, and may even develop a smug negative pride in having a problem the doctors cannot diagnose. The basic difficulty is not the doctor. He has been trained to work on the physical side of the human predicament, not on the spiritual side. He can cut out an inflamed appendix or give a shot of penicillin to control infection. But he does not know how to deal with aches and pains and feelings of apathy that come when a person is emotionally devastated and out of synchronization with the laws of God in his nature.

This concept of living in harmony with God's laws in nature and human nature explains why our lives are made or broken by our attitudes. I can't tell you how these laws work or even why, but I do know that affirmative attitudes determine what happens to us. And it is this set of attitudes, or our general attitude of continuing regard, that will make or break our lives. Jesus said, "I am come that they might have life, and that they might have it more abundantly" (John 10:10). This abundant life Jesus talks about is available to all of God's children who give themselves to the fullness of the presence of our risen Lord. Attitudes are habits of the mind. An attitude is a habitual way of thinking.

As our body is what we eat, our minds are what we think. And just as we can learn the discipline of positive control over our eating habits, we can also learn to control what goes into our minds. There are at least four sinful tendencies that will break our lives and leave all our hopes in shambles. Or, these tendencies can be transformed into attitudes to help fulfill God's purposes in our lives. These sinful tendencies include: (1) unresolved resentment, (2) self-pity, (3) unconfessed sin, and (4) a negative attitude. In their transformed state these tendencies become (1) forgiveness toward people who have hurt us, (2) a personal sense of self-worth, (3) the glory of forgiveness and cleansing, and (4) an affirming attitude toward life.

The Cancer of Resentment

Resentment is the basic problem which keeps most of us torn up on the inside. Jealousy without resentment is harmless enough. It may even foster a positive motivation. My nondestructive jealousy of your success may make me work harder. Anger without resentment is mostly an emotional release. Defeat without resentment is hardly a set-back. My defeat may become a time for regrouping. But resentment that feeds on the mind and claws at the emotions is doing the work of a cancer in the spirit.

The fact is that resentment does begin like a cancer. It is first small and imperceptible, suggesting little or no challenge to the normal functioning of the mind. Resentment may start with something someone said or something they should have said. Then comes some intrusion of injustice such as a blast of verbal abuse or human indignity, which triggers a flood of negative emotions that reproduce themselves out of control in the inner man like cancer does in the physical body. Then comes a succession of confirming incidents to convince us that the object of our resentment is the source of all our discomfort. There may be periods of remission when our minds are occupied with other challenges, but sooner or later we come back to times of brooding while the cancer continues its spread through the total personality, ultimately feeding on itself. Our resentment now has a life of its own.

Eventually, the cancer of the spirit grows so large everything else in our lives relates to it. All of the energy and drive we had formerly turned outward toward the goals of living are turned inward as we fight the battle for the life of our inner spirit. Slowly but inexorably the personality structure sags and deteriorates. We project all our problems on the person or the situation that has generated our consuming passion. Even in our moments of achievement we want to say, "If they could only see me now." The laurel wreath of triumph is withered by the scorching heat of unrelenting resentment.

No one is ever exempt from being the object of someone's resentment. We can have resentment against the person we sleep with every night of the world. We can have resentment against our most trusted friend, or our boss, or our most loyal employee. We can resent our pastor or a former pastor. It is highly possible to have resentment against one or more of our children. The coat of many colors fits any child who is the youngest, or most beautiful, or more appealing in the eyes of a parent. This unspoken partiality guarantees resentment in the sibling who feels left out. The parents who say they treat all of their children alike are admitting they don't, because no two children are alike, and therefore, each one must be treated individually. Resentment is like an influenza germ lurking in every relationship and can be activated with over-exposure to a series of chilly experiences. One of the sad facts about resentment is that most people do little or nothing to get rid of it. Most of us cultivate our negative emotions and keep our resentment alive as long as we can feel justified.

Justified Resentment

Larry Douglas had every visible reason to enjoy the fruits of happiness. Not yet forty, he was tall, good-looking, and financially comfortable, owning his own successful wholesale business. His house was beautiful. His wife was beautiful. They took vacations in exotic places. Their two lovely daughters, twelve and fifteen years of age, attended private schools. Besides the family car he had a sports car for himself. But—everything blew apart. His wife decided to divorce him on grounds of mental cruelty. She took the girls and moved from Oregon to California, leaving him with one of the most bitter cases of resentment I have ever known.

Larry took me to lunch one day and after the meal we sat in the parking lot while he poured out his story about all the things his ex-wife had done to him. He told me about her adulteries with only the slightest reference to the fact he might have had some of his own. He told me how she had blatantly talked about their problems to "everybody" in the church where they were both active members. He was angry with her reports that made him out to be at fault.

Finally I asked him: "Larry, do you realize what she is doing to you?"

Abruptly, Larry wheeled sideways in the bucket seat of his sports car and glared at me through eyes of fire. Suddenly I was an adversary. With exasperation he said, "Dr. Parrott, you just do not know *how justified I am to feel the way I feel.*" Then looking out through the windshield, he resumed his hostile exposé of her sins as though he were seeing invisible pictures of his wife's misdeeds.

Finally I stopped him. "Let's assume for a moment," I said, "that everything you have told me about your wife is fully true. However, if it is all true and then some, the fact remains that she is actually killing you. She has already destroyed the joy of your inner spirit and now she is working on the debilitation of your physical health. You did not eat your lunch. Before the afternoon is over you will need an antacid. You will drive this car aggressively to your plant, making you more susceptible to an accident. Before the day is done you are going to unload your frustrations on some of your employees, or worse, on some of your customers. And this evening you are going to drag yourself home, exhausted, to sit in an empty house and brood over all of the things this woman has done to you. Although she has moved a thousand miles away, she is actually destroying you."

It really does not matter how airtight our arguments are for justifying our most cherished resentments. The psychological and physical price for cultivating anger and keeping it alive is more than any of us can afford. And justified or not, the mental and physical results are the same. Unfortunately, the mind and the body do not know the difference between justified and unjustified resentment.

Resentment toward Dad

Resentment toward Mother or Father is a widespread virus. I know people who still harbor resentment toward their parents even after they are dead and gone. There are many adults with children of their own who still behave like Mother or Dad were judging their every move.

Mary was a twenty-six-year-old mother with two preschool daughters. I knew her as a child, lost contact, and then crossed paths with her in a Christian college where I was speaker for a chapel series. Mary was statuesque and handsome though not feminine enough to be considered beautiful. We hadn't talked long about former times until she abruptly shifted the subject and began to pour out some of the most vitriolic, pent-up words I had heard in a long time.

Mary's problem was her father. Her resentment against him was strong enough to color her whole life. She resented his generosity. "Sure, my dad gave more money than anyone else. He should. He's got more money than anybody else." Mary railed about her father's hypocrisy, which she saw as a gap between his devotion in church and the way he treated her and her mother at home. She blamed him for every bad experience she had ever had including her stormy six-year marriage that had ended in divorce. Resentment toward him was a provocation for her early marriage so she blamed her dad that it had turned sour. "I saw marriage as a way to get away from him and his domination." Even though her father was supporting her and the girls and paying the tuition she blamed him for the mess she was in. Now she was a single parent student trying to pick up on an interrupted education that she was sure would never have been interrupted if her father had not been the way he was. Just listening to her was an exhausting experience.

Mary and I made a lot of progress that week. She came to see her father, who was Prussian born, as a man who expressed his love by working hard to provide for his family. It was his austere manner that she contrasted to the American type of father who expresses his love with bountiful hugs and kisses while he takes time to be a supervisory playmate with his children. I really do believe she came to understand her father in a new and better light.

But I said, "Mary, I have a feeling that a better understanding of your father is not enough for you to let go of your resentment. It is still easier to blame him and keep your resentment alive than it is to forgive him for being himself. If you forgive him, then the consequences for your actions shift from him to you." And that is a radical shift for Mary, or any of us.

Mary did make an honest effort to forgive her father. We had a prayer together, which was the beginning of a new pilgrimage for her. Basic changes do not come in a miraculous moment standing alone as a quick external fix. The miraculous moment is more like a boundary we cross into an unknown field where we know the pearl of great price has been buried. I have kept in touch with Mary. She remarried and has moved around the country in connection with her husband's work. She has also developed a career of her own. And she has never gone back to the state of resentment against her father, at least not for long. Her progress has been in the right direction.

When I saw her pastor at a conference he volunteered this observation about her: "I have seen people saved from promiscuous sins. I have seen people saved from alcohol and drug addiction. I have even seen some tough characters saved from street crime. But never have I seen anyone as bitter and resentful as Mary who has become so loving and kind." Mary's transformation did not come in one magic moment while she waited passively for something to happen. Mary's transformation involved the connection between her will and God's grace.

The personality change many people need is not a face lift but a heart lift. The habit of happiness will not coexist with the habit of resentment. Learning to forgive the people who have hurt us will do more for our complexions than a carload of facial ointments. In every popular book on health and on every media talk show, the promise of a better life is made to those who exercise, eat properly, and take enough time for rest. But one more factor should be added to this glib prescription. Good physical and mental health also depends on our capacity to let forgiveness take the place of resentment.

Of all the people I can think of, no one was ever more justified in his feelings of resentment than Booker T. Washington. More than eighty years ago, he wrote his own story, *Up from Slavery*. He was born in the black ghetto on a white man's plantation in Franklin County, Virginia, in 1858 or 1859 (he never was really sure). By the time he could speak the language of his culture he was the victim of it. His crippling resentment would have been explained by modern

sociologists in terms of his negative environment. But somewhere during his growing up years, he transcended his natural self. As a young man he "resolved that because I had no
ancestry myself, I would leave a record of which my children
would be proud, and which might encourage them to still
higher effort."

But achievement for a black man was not easy in the years
following the Civil War. Abraham Lincoln gave the slaves
freedom, but he couldn't give them justice. However, Booker
T. Washington came to see his own problem as attitudinal,
not legal. He finally came to say with honesty, "I used to try
to picture in my imagination the feelings and ambitions of a
white boy with absolutely no limit placed on his aspirations
and activities. I used to envy the white boy who had no obstacles placed in his way of becoming a congressman, governor,
bishop or president by reason of his birth or race. I used to
picture the way I could act under the same circumstances,
how I would begin at the bottom and keep rising until I had
reached the highest round of success. In later years, I confess
that I do not envy the white boy as I once did. I have learned
that success is to be measured not so much by the position
one has reached in life as by the obstacles which he has
overcome in trying to succeed."

His achievements at the Tuskegee Institute and his research on the cultivation and commercial use of sweet pota-
toes and peanuts are legendary. But Booker T. Washington's
greatest legacy is himself as an example of a man who could
forgive the world for what it had done to him.

I hope I have made my point: Resentment is the cancer of
the inner spirit. It turns the challenge for achievement into a
struggle for existence and reduces enthusiasm to apathy.
When the tumors of resentment begin to grow, the habit of
happiness turns sour and the drive for life is reduced to a
crawl. On the other hand, freedom from resentment through
forgiveness is like a new vascular system after a heart by-pass.
There is no place for the affirmative life until resentment
is cleansed. Happiness and resentment will not mutually

coexist. And that is why we need to turn now to the process for cleansing our minds of resentment.

Discussion Questions:

1. What are some of the laws of God which hold this universe together and make it work?
2. What are the laws of God in human nature?
3. How are our lives made or broken by our attitudes?
4. In what ways is resentment a cancer?
5. Why does justification make no difference in the consequences of resentment?

Is any among you afflicted? let him pray. Is any merry? let him sing psalms (James 5:13).

Confess your faults one to another, and pray one for another, that ye may be healed. The effectual fervent prayer of a righteous man availeth much. Elijah was a man subject to like passions as we are, and he prayed earnestly that it might not rain: and it rained not on the earth by the space of three years and six months. And he prayed again, and the heaven gave rain, and the earth brought forth her fruit. Brethren, if any of you do err from the truth, and one convert him; let him know, that he which converteth the sinner from the error of his way shall save a soul from death, and shall hide a multitude of sins (James 5:16–20).

God cannot give us happiness and peace apart from himself, because it is not there.

C. S. Lewis

9

The Healing of Resentment

My life had every Christian advantage—or so it seemed. Our home was filled with stability and love. The very first memory I have of my mother and father is of them in church. I had to sit on my mother's lap because all the seats were needed for adults. My father stood behind the pulpit. As far back as I can recall I attended every service held on Sundays and weekdays, and I was enthusiastic about them all, especially the children's meetings.

Mrs. Rice was in charge of our Children's Church and she knew her stuff. We did not have videotapes, records, and sixteen-millimeter colored movies of Bible events, but we learned a solid set of biblical data, consisting of major passages for memorization such as Psalm 23 and the Beatitudes, plus the major Bible stories from the Old and New Testaments, names of the books of the Bible, how to find important passages, and a children's view of all the great Christian doctrines and basic principles for Christian living. When I was enrolled in a freshman college course on the Bible, I caught on quickly that my scope of Bible knowledge was ahead of most other students, thanks to good training in our church.

Another one of my childhood advantages was a mother who took it upon herself to read me the entire Egermier Bible

Story Book, a story a day. And we never finished a story until I was able to tell it back to her. Family prayers at our house were regularly attended. Our church had great revival meetings in those days, and all the famous evangelists ate dinner in our parsonage from time to time. They were my childhood heroes and friends. If it ever seemed like someone could get a satisfactory religious experience by absorbing the good atmosphere around him, it was I. All the theories about nurturing the Christian character should have worked in me if they were ever going to work. But somehow they did not.

Many secular theorists claim a child with too much exposure to religion will likely turn against it when he grows up. Certainly someone could have predicted a violent reaction by me against the religion of Mom and Dad because of the heavy restrictions they imposed. And, in many ways, there was provocation for revolt. As mentioned in a previous chapter, my parents would not let me attend the high school football games on Friday nights because of the distorted notions of some old ladies in our church who would have complicated my father's existence if he had allowed me to play in the marching band during the half-time show. Instead, I had to play my French horn in the high school orchestra. And I hated it. The band not only played at athletic events but they presented an annual concert in an auditorium called a "theatre." Many other restrictions like not drinking pop from a bottle and not playing card games followed the same bias based on the idea of shunning the very appearance of evil.

But my hang-ups were not those of the prodigal son whose resentment drove him into a far country. I was never tempted to run away, or to see what the other side of life was like. Pornography and drugs and all they represent were not in our scene. I lived comfortably within the limits of the written as well as the unwritten law of both the church and the home.

My problems became those of the self-righteous older brother, the good guy who stayed home and behaved himself. Dante was right when he placed the sins of the spirit in the hottest regions of hell. There is no fire that burns whiter on the inside of a man than the flames of self-righteousness and self-pity.

My self-righteousness evolved into a negative fascination with *inconsistencies* in the lives of people who attended church regularly. I was not able to handle the obvious contradictions in the lives of people who claimed to be spiritual.

There was the unlovable old gentleman in our church who came to the parsonage and spoke disrespectfully to my father, the Sunday school teacher who called me "a smart aleck" when I asked him for the dime he promised for each new boy we brought, the church lay leader who put me down over something I could not help or change. In later years a series of unfortunate events contrived to fuel the fires of resentment that finally blazed into the white heat of bitterness. Without realizing it, I became a cynic. In my outward piety I chose to be hurt easily and then responded with blazing, self-righteous judgment, which surfaced most often in fault-finding and self-pity. My continuing attitude could be described as critical, censorious, negative, bitter, and self-defeating.

At one point I became a specialist in the inconsistencies and weaknesses of the church. The discipline, the doctrinal statement, and the organizational and governmental procedures, which had been hammered out on the anvils of scripture, human experience, corporate conscience, logic, and the democratic processes of general assembly, were the objects of my scorn. The theological alternatives to our family faith I explored with intense interest and hope for a better way. However, I found the lack of biblical authority in one wing of Protestantism and the rational legalism in another wing less satisfactory to me than the experience-centered theology of my own church.

It would seem that these academic forays into alternative theologies would have had a settling effect, but they did not. Intellectual light did not illuminate the dark places in my spirit. Frustrated by the people I let hurt me and the church I could not easily dismiss, the next step toward my spiritual dead-end was self-hate, which became enormous when I turned all my frustrated energies inward against myself. Jealousy, resentment, and self-pity spread like ugly weeds in a garden with good soil previously sown with good seed.

The symptoms of my negative spirit were predictable: My feelings were too easily hurt. I was destroyed inwardly by my contradictory feelings of inadequacy and the compensating factor of a show of self-confidence. Other people's successes fired the smoldering confusion and misunderstanding within me. I spoke rudely to people if the risk of their retaliation was low. I gave every conversation a critical turn. Hurt invited hurt like the magnet that draws the slivers of steel. Tears of pure anguish flowed out of dead-end desperation.

Then my life did a turn-around. It was not a quick fix from outside myself that, in a magic moment, solved all my attitudinal problems. No. It began with a moment of emotional decision making that provided the turning point, or the turn-around, from a negative way of thinking to a new affirming lifestyle. This was the beginning for my habit of happiness. It happened on a Monday night in Salem, Oregon, by the side of the bed in the low-rent, second-floor apartment where my wife, Lora Lee, and I lived while I was enrolled in graduate school. We had attended a service earlier in the evening. The speaker was an excellent preacher, and the pastor of our church was a great person. But they were not the agents of my turn-around.

During the meeting, as we sat in a forward pew near the front on the right side of the sanctuary next to the wall, I came to the end of myself. All at once I came to see myself as I really was—self-centered, bitter, fault-finding, hurt, jealous, full of self-pity. All at once I realized that my problem was not other people, but myself, not somebody out there, but me on the inside. I had run out of time if I expected to put my life together, and I knew it. The only hope for me was a whole new beginning with a new set of motives and attitudes that could change my way of thinking about people and about myself. I suppose I would have responded to an invitation hymn if one had been sung, but there was none. And it was just as well, for this decision was a private matter.

Back in the apartment, I knelt by the side of the bed with my Bible open before me. I was so miserable I never even thought to pray for Lora Lee who knelt beside me. A better theological understanding was not my concern as I told God how miserable I was—as if he did not know. I confessed all the negative habits of thinking I had developed and nurtured. I accepted responsibility for my state of mind, which was a big step for me, since I had always blamed other people for my problems. I asked forgiveness for the way I had put down my detractors. I told God I believed in the truth of New Testament faith even if no one lived it.

Putting people on the altar of my heart, never to judge them again, was a gigantic step for me. I could see what was wrong with almost anyone. Finally, I told the Lord I knew his spirit could cleanse all that needed to be cleansed and the full presence of the Holy Spirit could renew my mind and take over my life. Without any real begging or pleading, I just waited for his presence to come, and he did. I have heard other people talk about great feelings overwhelming them in a life-changing experience, but I did not really have any great feelings. Mostly I just had a deep, abiding confidence that from now on everything was going to be different because I would be headed in a new direction.

And it has been different, so different that I seldom go to Salem, Oregon, without taking time to drive by the apartment where my life made its turn-around.

The external factors in life have not been that different. Life still has its bumps, its low spots, inequities, and inconsistencies. Life is not always fair. But from then until now, I have worked at developing a set of attitudes that make the habit of happiness an ongoing possibility. Sometimes it seems I have lived a charmed life because wonderful opportunities and experiences have come to Lora Lee and me that we would not have dared to dream. For instance, I would never have dared to think about being president of my alma mater, the same college where my father was president thirty years before me. I would not go back to the former negativism for anything in the world.

People still take occasion to complicate my existence, but when they do, it is wonderful to see how God works. Each stage of life has its own unique challenges and problems. But since the day I died to the old way of thinking and living, many years ago, my new life in Christ has never been tarnished by a lapse from the habit of happiness into the old negativism. The problems I create myself, and the ones others create for me, and the ones created for me by circumstances are not signs of failure in the affirmative life but just segments in my pilgrimage.

For me to reduce to prescription what happened to me through the renewing of my attitudes would be a contradiction of the process. An oversimplified analysis, complete with neat categories, results in what has been called the tyranny of the formula. There is a tailor-made quality about renewal which is unique to each person. And reductionism is the peril of those who philosophize. However, I have observed several steps that seem to be part of every man's experience as well as my own, as we face in ourselves the unresolved problems of resentment.

Trace It Back

As a starting point for people who want to change, we need to *trace our resentment if possible back to its source*. This is not easy. When any of us has resentment toward another person, we feel that individual has always been bad and we are smart enough to catch on to this deviousness. But resentment always has a beginning.

Since each person is a mixture of good and bad, something in the relationship of two or more people brings out the worst in each—and resentment is the result on one or all sides. Sometimes this negative turning point in the relationship is the result of competition. Since everyone wants to be a winner, it is easy to build resentment toward those who have successfully prevailed against us. Or, resentment can begin with the simple fact that some people, by their physical presence, make us feel more inadequate. They intimidate us. They may not take enough time to recognize us adequately, or they fail to be sensitive in saying and doing the things that enhance our self-image. Then, in some cases of resentment we have been put down in a way that leaves a permanent hurt smoldering and burning. Or, resentment may have been kindled by a situation in which the other person was simply doing his job as he saw it, but the results came down hard against us, and we reacted.

I once paid a big price to attend a seminar in a famous hotel in Philadelphia, where we were promised practical help in how to build good relationships with the people we count on in our work. After two days of generally excellent material and superior teaching, the professor said all that we had paid for could be reduced to just one sentence: *We build good relationships with people when we have the sensitivity and the will to reinforce their values.* When we fail to be sensitive to the value system of others and go roughshod over the things they believe in, we are likely to generate hostility instead of gratitude. But regardless of how resentment starts, it is helpful to trace it back to its beginning.

Talk It Out

Second, it helps in dealing with your resentment to find a nonjudgmental person with whom you can talk out the problem. Carl Rogers, the famous counseling psychologist, wrote, "God has made man so he can gain insight into his own problem *if* he can articulate that problem in a nonjudgmental atmosphere." James, the brother of Jesus, wrote to the embattled Christians under the heel of Rome in first century Jerusalem, "Confess your faults one to another . . . that ye may be healed" (James 5:16).

The trouble with the advice from Carl Rogers and James is the difficulty in finding a nonjudgmental person. One study of grade school children demonstrates how hard it is to find people we can trust with our problems. These children seldom talked out their real problems with the teacher for fear of the consequences. And, of course, they never talked with the principal because he or she was even a greater threat as an authority figure. And furthermore, the principal might telephone Mother or Dad. To the surprise of the investigators, they learned that the children turned most often to the school custodian. The janitor could be trusted to listen without judging. Sometimes he rewarded the children with a piece of candy or some other symbol of acceptance after they had finished telling their woes.

It might seem the most logical person to confess to is the past And in the Catholic church systematic provision is made for confession. But even in the confessional, the idea of penance is usually attached to expiation. In Protestant churches the pastor is often the counselor of the flock. More and more pastors are receiving special training for this phase of their ministry. Many of them keep regular office hours for confession and discussion. But many laymen will never go to their pastor because of their fear that confessing the truth may lead the pastor to think less of them. They may even fear the possibility of becoming an illustration in next Sunday's sermon. And unforgivably, there have been times when pastors have not kept their professional commitment to total secrecy in what they have heard from parishioners.

There is a school of psychiatric thought which says every "normal person" is one who has at least one other individual to whom he or she can go and talk things out, telling it like it is without fear of recrimination or misuse of the shared information. And the "abnormal person" is one who has gone for a lifetime without ever developing one relationship with another human being to talk to without fear.

If necessary, anyone of us can go to a professional counselor, and for a reasonable sum, have an attentive listener who can ask appropriate leading questions and guide us through a helpful catharsis. This is a good and live option. But I have another idea. I really believe the person God intended us to have as our confessor, when he organized the world into families, is one's husband or wife. It is great to have a relation-ship with our spouse that can stand the force of an outpour-ing of pent-up emotion without fear of a shouting match, judgmental retaliation, or a reaction of disinterest. There is powerful therapy in talking out our unresolved problems of resentment with a sensitive, understanding spouse who will listen and not judge us because of his or her love for us.

Turn It Over

Third is the need to commit the problem into the hands of God. Even if we are unable to find a person with whom we can talk out our unresolved resentment, there is still hope. We must finally commit our resentments to God. Positive things in life, such as talents, or money, or family, may be consecrated to God for his service. But broken relationships with people, emotions damaged by unhealthy competition, and memories that harbor hurt need to be committed, not consecrated. Resentment is not useful to God or to ourselves. It needs to be washed away.

Mahatma Gandhi and Martin Luther King did not have their greatest struggles with the oppressive systems they fought, but with their own resentment. Before they were ready to do the positive work of healing among their people, they had to be healed themselves. They were not ready to lead their people until first they had committed all of the inequities, brutalities, and the abuse of the sheer, raw power of their enemies into the hands of God. A nonviolent relation-ship with our oppressors is not possible as long as we are still dominated by debilitating resentments.

Make It Work

The next and final step in getting rid of resentment is to reprogram the mind. After resentment is traced back, talked out, and turned over, there is still one step left in being rid of it. We must learn how to think acceptable thoughts about the objects of our resentment, whoever or whatever they may be. After resentments have been turned over to God, it is time to program a new set of attitudes into the brain. This is the time to exchange our unresolved resentments for the habit of happiness.

The most basic type of propaganda is card-stacking. When we stack the cards to favor a person, we go through his life experiences lifting out every good and acceptable characteristic that we can fortify with anecdotes and the testimony of witnesses, while we ignore the bad things. And if we need to stack the cards against someone, we go through his life picking out every miserable negative factor we can use against him as we try to hide the good qualities. Every resentful person in the world uses the technique of card-stacking against the people they resent. Anything their detractor does well is discounted. If anything noteworthy is achieved, we call it luck, or we accuse them of conniving and scheming. And when we hear reports of failure among the people we resent, we gleefully conclude they got what they deserved.

These negative reactions against people we resent have been programmed into our minds. Negative reactions are like the reflexes built into the nervous system. The reflexes of the involuntary nervous system work without thought. The eyelid flutters instinctively to avoid dust in the eye bypassing the cognitive processes of thinking. Even after we have been cleansed of a resentful attitude by talking it out and taking it to God, our minds are still programmed negatively against the people we resented. Our negative inclinations have been deeply ingrained and seemingly respond involuntarily. It takes an exercise of our will to deprogram these negative inclinations. Each time we start to bring a negative mental picture into focus, or place an unkind word on our tongue, or respond to a critical surge, we simply command ourselves to stop and replace the mental picture, the emotional surge, or the negative thought with a realistically positive observation. We accept the fact that each human being, including ourselves, is a mixture of good and bad. No one is perfect. No one is totally good or bad. We learn to assent to the good and bad within ourselves as the basis for accepting the other person who is also a bundle of contradictions, but worthy of our love and understanding.

I am often asked if it is necessary to apologize to the person we have resented. Actually there is no unqualified "yes" or "no" to this question. If we apologize to some people, they take our apology as a sign of weakness and move harder against us. With other people, a word fitly spoken may be like "apples of gold and pitchers of silver." More likely than not, it is better to skip the apology and send out a set of positive signals toward the person against whom we have had resentment. It often helps to take the lead in little gestures like meeting together for coffee. It can never hurt to make a point of speaking a kind word when the name of the formerly resented person comes up in conversation. The message of our changed attitude will fly on the wireless of human chemistry when we begin sending out the signals. Given enough time, an affirming attitude will almost always evoke a positive response. A new relationship is much more important than a wimpy apology. However, if an apology will help give birth to a new and improved relationship then try it.

Discussion Questions:

1. What explanation is there for the person who seems to attract all the bad "luck" while others go successfully along their way?

2. What are the four sinful tendencies indicated in this chapter?

3. In what ways does resentment work like a cancer?

4. What happens to us when we feel our resentment is justified?

5. What place is there for religious experience in the transformation of our resentments into forgiveness?

6. What are the four phases in changing a bad attitude?

Truly God is good to Israel, even to such as are of a clean heart. But as for me, my feet were almost gone; my steps had well-nigh slipped. For I was envious at the foolish, when I saw the prosperity of the wicked. For there are no bands in their death: but their strength is firm. They are not in trouble as other men; neither are they plagued like other men. Therefore pride compasseth them about as a chain; violence covereth them as a garment. Their eyes stand out with fatness: they have more than heart could wish. They are corrupt, and speak wickedly concerning oppression: they speak loftily. They set their mouth against the heavens, and their tongue walketh through the earth . . . Behold these are the ungodly, who prosper in the world; they increase in riches. Verily I have cleansed my heart in vain, washed my hands in innocency. For all the day long have I been plagued, and chastened every morning . . . When I thought to know this, it was too painful for me; until I went into the sanctuary of God; then understood I their end. Surely thou didst set them in slippery places: thou castedst them down into destruction . . . Whom have I in heaven but thee? And there is none upon earth that I desire besides thee (Psalm 73:1–9, 12–14, 16–18, 25).

It is not how much we have, but how much we enjoy, that makes happiness.

Charles Haddon Spurgeon

10

Self-Pity

During my years at Michigan State University there was a professor, Dr. Ernest O. Milby, who made a difference in my life. He had the ability to speak without notes for an hour and a half to a sophisticated class of graduate students who gave him a standing ovation at the end of his lecture. I never saw this happen with anyone else. As both a model and a teacher, he helped me understand for the first time, and more than any other person I have known, the amazing power of our attitudes.

But of all I learned from Dr. Milby, one concept has irreversibly stuck in my mind. First of all, he told us to take our Ph.D. diplomas and stick them in the bottom of a trunk and forget we ever had them except as credentials for getting a job. Then he warned us again and again that "self-pity is the luxury you cannot afford." He strongly directed us to reconsider our career, and take seriously the option of resigning whatever job we had if we found our enthusiasm was gone and we were beginning to feel sorry for ourselves. He made it clear to me, in a way I have never forgotten, that no one can ever be an effective human being, marriage partner, parent, or career person if he has to take on the emotional overload of self-pity. Any amount of self-pity is more than enough.

Self-pity has nothing to do with circumstances. It is a frame of mind. The person who is best trained or most poorly educated in our circle of friends can be filled with self-pity. I have known men and women who were highly successful in their careers who felt sorry for themselves because they had failed to make the last promotion, or felt that promotions were coming too slowly. And this self-pity was the beginning of their long slide down or out, or both. All of us have seen the contradiction in the rich who complain about paying taxes when they might well be grateful they have an income to be taxed. Self-pity is not determined by our circumstances; it is a way of thinking.

Some years ago my secretary ushered in a tall, striking lady, impeccably dressed, who was carrying a bundle of letters in envelopes tied together with a red ribbon. After the lady left, my secretary suggested I might want to step out into the foyer to see the automobile she was driving. It was a hand-tooled convertible costing more than most men would make in several years. She had the top down. Her powder-blue jacket matched the color of her car. She was wearing sunglasses and had long peroxide blonde hair that fell across her shoulders in a studied informality. She was a classy lady who could slow the flow of traffic.

The first thing this lady did, when she came into my office, was to place a generous check on my desk. I thanked her and said the check would go into the offering plate of our church. Then she handed me her package of letters and wanted me to untie the red ribbon and read them. I countered with the suggestion that we talk awhile first.

In only minutes it was apparent that a great part of her problem was an overwhelming sense of self-pity. She told me how she and her husband had lived together in a small, comfortable bungalow on the south side of Kansas City. She said her husband was a trouble-shooter for a large printing plant and a genius in maintaining and operating its machinery. She knew he traveled often but never asked any questions because she understood he was going about his work maintaining the printing presses for the company in several cities. He came home each week with a paycheck, which was given directly to her. And with a fairly small amount of money returned to him for buying lunches, she looked after the household, felt fulfilled, and was happy in her relationship with him. A working man's check was good enough for them to enjoy their style of life.

Then one Saturday he worked all day and, after leaving for home at night, was hit broadside by a drunk driver and killed instantly. When they got into his affairs, she learned her husband was not a millwright employed by a printing company. He actually owned, outright, six of the largest printing plants in the United States. She was an instant multi-millionaire, many times over. As the tears streamed across her face she told me how miserable life had become since she inherited her millions, and how she longed for the earlier days when life was simple and her role was clearly defined. She was feeling sorry for herself even though she had what many other people would give their lives for. I never did get to read the letters!

I wish I could say that self-pity is related primarily to money. But it is not. Some of the best people I have ever known, even ministers, have been afflicted and permanently damaged by self-pity. One afternoon my wife and I pulled into the driveway of a minister friend who came from his parsonage to greet us before we ever got out of the car. He quickly passed the minimal civilities of the greeting and burst into a story of self-pity concerning the assignment the church hierarchy had given him. He told me how the congregation had been misrepresented to him, was a setback in his ministerial career, and consisted of people who were not as well educated and materially successful as he was. He saw himself as a man for the First Church of the Middle Class, feeling sorry for himself because he was forced to pastor a blue-collar congregation.

As we drove away from his home later that afternoon, I said to my wife that it was going to be most interesting to see what happened to a man so thoroughly consumed with self-pity.

Even though he was, in many ways, a good and godly man, he had been mortally hurt by a self-inflicted wound. He had been poisoned by the distortions of his own mind. Within a year this clergyman had resigned his church and announced his intention to do specialized itinerant preaching. When it became clear there was not enough demand for his services to keep himself busy in free-lance work, he left the ministry and became a public school teacher. Not long ago I picked up a church periodical and saw an announcement about him in the obituary column. He had passed away at a comparatively young age. I showed the death notice to my wife and asked, "Do you think he would have died if he had been able to overcome his self-pity and live with an affirming outlook?"

She said, "No," and I agreed with her.

I once had a friend in Seattle named Mrs. McDonald, the mother-in-law of the famous best-selling authoress, Betty McDonald. If ever I knew a woman who had a right to be filled with self-pity, she did. In one six-month period she had enough happen to her to utterly devastate most people. First of all, her husband died. This was bad enough but worse because he left her less than penniless. She was in debt with a backlog of monthly bills. Three months after the funeral, she was in an automobile accident that mutilated her legs and led a team of doctors to make a decision to cut off one leg at the hip to save her life. Three months later the same doctors decided the other leg had to be severed, or she would die. And within a six-month period, she wound up a penniless widow, in debt, with both legs gone. This would have been enough to destroy most women, but not Mrs. McDonald.

She got a carpenter to build a small elevator which could carry her from the sidewalk up an incline to the back door of her hillside house. The same carpenter was instructed to cut down the height of the cabinets in the kitchen and to build extensions on the working areas to accommodate her wheelchair. This made it possible for her to prepare meals and do other kitchen work. Next, she had to decide what to do for a living. Realizing most options were closed to her, she decided the only realistic thing she could do was to start a telephone sales business. And she did.

I have known of people in Seattle who called Mrs. McDonald to buy things they might have bought somewhere else, just because the sales exchange gave them an opportunity to absorb a little of her sunshine. The last time she ever came to hear me speak, she rode across Seattle in a taxicab. I borrowed an automobile and took her home that night. We rode together up the little elevator, toured the house and sales facilities tailor-made for her wheelchair. Then we sat in her living room while she inspired me with story after story of how good God was and how great it was to be alive.

When I left the home of Mrs. McDonald and returned to my hotel room, I tried to analyze what makes some people rise above self-pity while others are the victims of it. The research has not yet been done and the book has not yet been written on the dynamics of self-pity. But more than 2500 years ago a wise man in the Middle East wrote a Hebrew poem in which he clearly outlined, at least for me and many others who have read it, the dynamics of overcoming self-pity.

King David knew the temptations to self-pity personally. After Goliath was killed, King Saul turned against the warrior with a sling-shot. Although Saul was a victor over the friends of Goliath he became the victim of his own jealousy and self-pity. It seemed like Saul set out to prove the saying of the cynics: "No good deed ever goes unpunished." Saul tried to run David through with a javelin. He almost nailed David to the wall. This was only the beginning of sorrows that did not appease Saul's jealousy and self-pity until he finally fell on his own sword.

David also knew the anger that turns into self-pity when a man is caught in the sins of adultery and attempts a cover-up. He also knew what it was to have a son turn against him and use every scheming device he could to destroy his father's leadership and run him from office. But in spite of hard times and bitter personal experiences, David was able to lead Israel through its golden age. There is no easy way to transform the sour wine of self-pity into the elixir of self-healing. But there are guidelines in this ancient psalm that have the clinical ring of a modern solution.

The Therapy of Stillness

David characterized the problem of self-pity better than most modern writers when he said, "Truly God is good . . . But as for me, my feet were almost gone, my steps had well-nigh slipped. For I was envious of the foolish, when I saw the prosperity of the wicked. For there are no bands in their death . . . They are not in trouble . . . pride compasseth them about . . . Their eyes stand out with fatness: they have more than heart could wish. They are corrupt, and speak wickedly . . . They set their mouth against the heavens, and their tongue walketh through the earth" (Psalm 73:1–9).

Then David came to the therapy of stillness as the first step in overcoming self-pity. "When I thought to know this it was too painful for me *until I went into the sanctuary of God.*" God's sanctuary may be a Gothic cathedral or the color-coordinated auditorium of an evangelical church. God's sanctuary is anywhere you and I stop long enough to meet him. It may be at the top of a ski-run, along a mountain stream, in a boat, on our knees at the divan in the family room, or lying awake in the darkest hours of the night. But people who learn to deal with self-pity first learn the therapy of stillness. We can't hear what God says until we stop long enough to listen, and we cannot listen until we become still enough to hear him.

Sitting quietly in church is a spiritual experience even if the service is but minimally helpful. The late Bishop Kennedy of the Methodist church said a man who came regularly to his services and seemed to listen receptively told him not to be flattered by his systematic attendance. The man said he had a hectic job that pulled him in many directions all week long. "On Sunday," he said, "it does me good to dress up and come to this sanctuary for an hour. If the sermon is good I am always glad but if it is not, the hour of quietness always does me good anyhow." And he might have added, "With a week like mine, I need the quietness of a church like yours."

There was a time when I fretted over dull, uninteresting services, but not anymore. I've come to accept the therapy of the soul that comes when we turn off the engine, stop talking, and sit still. With my Bible open before me, it is amazing what God has to say to me even if the sermon has not captured my attention.

The therapy of stillness comes in our private time for prayer and meditation. It was a good day for me when I learned prayer was not a monologue. Sometimes it is a conversation. But it is always a time to relax, to sit still or kneel, and hear what God wants to say to us. If God speaks to us through the subconscious then quietness is the conduit through which his voice often passes. I don't think of myself as mystical. My religion is far too practical for that. But I would not exchange the moments of quietness each day for any two consecutive meals. When the phone stops and the secretary is busy at her work, I can close the door at least once each day and sit quietly with my Bible and my heart open to God. And when I do he always has something to say. At that moment, my office has become the sanctuary of God.

The Long Look

When David stopped to think about the reasons for his self-pity, he began to realize that the collage of life consists of more than a few candid shots of the wicked in their moments of triumph. He said, "Surely thou didst set them in slippery places" (Psalm 73:18). David's statement implies the long look at life. The embezzler is rich for the moment, and the manipulations of the conniver may be successful at the time. And there is nothing like the pride of a poor man who has hit it rich and thinks he did it on his own. But in life, it is the long pull which matters.

There is the parable of the infidel in a small Kansas town who mounted a soapbox in front of the county courthouse and declared to the people, "There is no God, and I will prove it to you." Then in a demonstration of arrogant ignorance he continued with a great flourish of his hand toward the sky as he looked upward and cried, "If there be a God let him strike me dead." When nothing happened he turned haughtily to the people and laughingly said, "See! I told you there is no God. If there were a God, he would never stand for me to defy him without striking back." In the small group who heard the infidel that day was the editor of the town's weekly paper. He went back to his office, wrote an open letter to the infidel, and published it in the next edition. And, among other things, he reminded him that "God does not collect all of his debts in the month of September."

One of the things I like about the elderly is their long look at life. They have seen enough to know that very little is new, only different. Today's new style is yesterday's discard. Whatever comes, they know by experience, will also pass. They've seen long hair and short hair, long skirts and short skirts, the Beatles and the be-boppers, big cars and small cars, and whatever else comes down the pike. They have been through periods of war, peace, apathy, depression, high interest, low interest, bank failures, national turmoil, and a plethora of other times, experiences, fads, and crises. They have learned life goes on and very few of the issues that burn up people's energies and sidetrack their purposes are worth what they demand from us.

It would be wonderful if we could learn to put life in perspective without waiting until we grow old. Most of the people at the top are, as David said, "in slippery places." The first really big entrepreneur who impressed me and captured my imagination was William Zeckendorf, who bought the Chrysler Building along with dozens of expensive mid-town Manhattan properties. He set developments in place with price tags that blew my mind. But just as I decided he was smart enough to be invincible I picked up the *New York Times* and read on the front page that he was going bankrupt.

In the harbor of Monte Carlo I saw a huge ocean-going yacht so impressive I asked who owned it. Someone said it belonged to Khashoggi, who was probably the richest man in the world. The spoils of his many enterprises have afforded him twelve homes spread around the globe, including one in the bushveldt of Africa. Each of these world-wide homes contained telephones with direct lines for dialing local calls in New York City, even from the hinterlands of Africa. I was really impressed until I read in the European edition of the *New York Herald Tribune* that Khashoggi had fallen on hard times because of the drop in oil prices and was selling his yacht to help recover his losses.

David knew what we all need to learn: that all of the successes in life are "in slippery places." There are some happy rungs on the ladder besides the one at the top. Titles and positions come and go like the tides of the sea, but life, like the oceans, keeps rolling on.

Self-pity Only Hurts Ourselves

David saw the error of his own attitude when he wrote, "Thus my heart was grieved, and I was pricked in my reins. So foolish was I" (Psalm 73:21–22). Wisdom for overcoming self-pity has peaked when we become aware of what it does to us. But with this awareness must come a willingness to stop feeling sorry for ourselves and to change the way we think about ourselves. As David implies, no person is forced to be foolish. It is a personal decision.

The heart of this Psalm is the foolishness of David's self-pity when he compared his situation with successes of the evil men around him. Here is what he saw in them:

(1) *"Their strength is firm."* The strength of strong people can make fools like you and me feel inadequate and drop out of the race.

(2) *"They are not in trouble."* Have you ever been stopped by a policeman when you knew other people had been more guilty of speeding than yourself? You were just trying to pass an obstinate trucker. It's hard to pay that kind of fine and keep smiling.

(3) *"They have more than a heart could wish."* Mr. Leonard Spangenburg, the President of Babson, told me the most exaggerated figure in the world is the other man's net worth. It is easy to feel sorry for ourselves when we compare what we know we have to what we think someone else has.

(4) *"They are corrupt and speak wickedly."* Self-pity can get a fast start in the mind of a struggling student who has passed up opportunities for dishonesty while watching other students cheat and get away with it, even bragging about it in the college hang-out.

All of David's comparisons, designed to trigger self-pity, were too much for him. "When I thought to know this it was too painful for me." The pain of self-pity is inflicted on ourselves and is designed to hurt no one but us. The manufacturer of thoughts filled with self-pity consumes his own product and suffers all the related pains. Self-pity is a self-destructive characteristic that does not deserve to exist. Why do we punish ourselves with self-pity when the pain is not necessary?

Discussion Questions:

1. Why is self-pity a luxury none of us can afford?
2. What opportunities do you have for the therapy of stillness?
3. What is the long look at life?
4. Why is self-pity foolish?
5. What successes did David see in sinful men?

Have mercy upon me, O God, according to thy loving-kindness: according unto the multitude of thy tender mercies blot out my transgressions. Wash me thoroughly from mine iniquity, and cleanse me from my sin. For I acknowledge my transgressions: and my sin is ever before me. Against thee, thee only, have I sinned, and done this evil in thy sight: that thou mightest be justified when thou speakest, and be clear when thou judgest. Behold, I was shapen in iniquity; and in sin did my mother conceive me. Behold, thou desirest truth in the inward parts: and in the hidden part thou shalt make me to know wisdom. Purge me with hyssop, and I shall be clean: wash me, and I shall be whiter than snow. Make me to hear joy and gladness; that the bones which thou has broken may rejoice. Hide thy face from my sins, and blot out all mine iniquities. Create in me a clean heart, O God; and renew a right spirit within me. Cast me not away from thy presence; and take not thy Holy Spirit from me. Restore unto me the joy of thy salvation; and uphold me with thy free spirit. Then will I teach transgressors thy ways; and sinners shall be converted unto thee. Deliver me from bloodguiltiness, O God, thou God of my salvation: and my tongue shall sing aloud of thy righteousness. O Lord, open thou my lips; and my mouth shall show forth thy praise. For thou desirest not sacrifice; else would I give it: thou delightest not in burnt offering. The sacrifices of God are a broken spirit: a broken and a contrite heart, O God, thou wilt not despise. Do good in thy good pleasure unto Zion: build thou the walls of Jerusalem. Then shalt thou be pleased with the sacrifices of righteousness, with burnt offering and whole burnt offering: then shall they offer bullocks upon thine altar (Psalm 51).

There is no duty we so much underrate as the duty of being happy.

Robert Louis Stevenson
An Apology for Idlers

11

Confession and Restitution

Sin is an important theological word but also a sound psychological concept. Here's why: It is impossible to live a radiant, happy, productive life with guilt beneath the surface. Even when the causes of our guilt have been submerged in the dark recesses of the subconscious, the emotional consequences keep on working.

The famous psychologist, C. Hudson Herrick, has written that ignorance, immaturity, and willful transgression of the laws of man's nature are inevitably punished. "Transgression of these laws brings its own penalty. No prosecutor is required. If you drink whiskey to excess, your health is impaired. If you drink wood alcohol, you die . . . the wages of sin is death, if not of the person, certainly of his richest values and satisfactions. And ignorance of the law excuses no man."

Dr. O. Hobart Mowrer of the University of Illinois said in his book, *Crisis in Psychiatry and Religion,* "The major problem with man today is the problem of guilt. And by this I do not mean the nebulous guilt feelings of the psychiatrist but of plain, objective guilt which comes when we break the laws of God in human nature."

Dr. Karl A. Menninger, in *Whatever Happened to Sin?*, explains the evolution of the biblical concept of sin. When the laws relating to sin were separated out from the Bible they were codified in the civil laws of the land. From the law books, sin was relocated in the environment, which is held responsible for most antisocial behavior these days. In summary he says guilt is guilt and sin is sin. And the only solution for both is in forgiveness and cleansing.

Sin is both attitude and action, the will of the mind and the behavior of the body. Sin is commonly defined by theologians as willful acts, or acts against the laws of God. John Wesley focused on personal responsibility when he said, "Sin is a willful transgression against a known law of God." Even the broader definition of sin as "missing the mark" implies doing something inherently wrong. Therefore we see sin in such actions as lying, stealing, and adultery. In civil law these actions are declared wrong because of their antisocial character. In God's law these actions are wrong because they go against the nature of man as God created him. For instance, lesbianism, homosexuality, and adultery are not right or wrong on the basis of laws legislated by representatives of the people. These practices are not right or wrong because of the laws on the books in the capital. Homosexuality and lesbianism are not wrong because the Bible said so. The Bible says they are wrong because they go against the nature of man as originally created: "For this cause God gave them up unto vile affections: for even their women did change the natural use into that which is against nature: And likewise also the men, leaving the natural use of the woman, burned in their lust one toward another; men with men . . ." (Romans 1:26-27). Then Paul continued his exposé of sin by concluding there is "the righteous judgment of God . . . Who will render to every man according to his deeds" (Romans 2:5-6). No legislation on the behavior of consenting adults can change the emotional, physical, and spiritual consequences of deeds against the spirit of the body.

But sin is not only action that misses the mark or is antisocial in nature; sin is also an attitude. Back of every lie, or theft, or adultery, or murder is a thought. And when these thoughts, which result in sinful actions, become habits of the mind they have become attitudes. An attitude is a habitual way of thinking. This is why Jesus taught that the sin of lust is in the mind before it ever becomes a physical act. "Whosoever looketh on a woman to lust after her hath committed adultery with her already in his heart" (Matthew 5:28).

The most descriptive passage on sinful attitudes in the Bible comes from the pen of St. Paul in Romans 1. In describing the people "God gave over to a reprobate mind," he lists a great number of sins:

Unrighteousness	Haters of God
Fornication	Despitefulness
Wickedness	Proud
Covetousness	Boasters
Maliciousness	Inventors of evil things
Envy	Disobedient to parents
Murder	Without understanding
Debate	Covenant breakers
Deceit	Without natural affection
Malignity	Implacable
Whisperers	Unmerciful
Backbiters	

Some of these sins focus on evil acts such as fornication, murder, and covenant breaking. Other sins focus more on attitudes such as covetousness, maliciousness, and envy. But every sin in Paul's list includes both thought and action. From sinful attitudes come sinful acts. The most depraved person is the one whose mind is most dominated by evil attitudes.

Understanding the connection between sinful attitudes and sinful acts is not enough. Knowledge, of itself, does not take away sin. Besides faith in the finished work of our Lord, it seems to me there are two important considerations for people who want psychological as well as theological and spiritual victory over sin. These two factors are confession and restitution.

Confession

The superintendent of nurses in a large hospital phoned me one day about a young lady she said would be sent home from nursing school unless something could be done to effect a radical change in her. She said the student had unprovoked crying spells. She was unhappy with the second roommate in the same term and wanted to make a change. The superintendent said the student could not concentrate and her anger was on a hair trigger. She would blow up at the slightest provocation. Worst of all, she flunked her last examination. Finally, the nursing superintendent said, "I am going to be forced to send her home unless something can be done soon." She asked me if I would talk with the young lady, and I agreed.

When the nursing student arrived she sat across my desk glumly looking at me with distrust and resistance. Finally I stopped her fumbling efforts to talk and suggested it was not useful for her or me to go on with the conversation. She had only come because the superintendent had sent her. She didn't know me, or trust me, or even like me. I suggested she leave and come again if she wished on another day, or if she never came back that would be her decision. It was tough love, but it worked.

Two days later the young lady showed up unannounced, sat in the same chair, and began talking, carefully choosing her words. After some fifteen or twenty minutes of skirting the issues, she suddenly straightened up, looked at me sharply, and wanted to know if the gadgets on my desk were turned on. When I said "No," she wanted to know if I would tell the superintendent of nurses anything she would tell me. Again I said, "No." And with this assurance she launched into a story of confession. Her confession must have gone on for eight or ten minutes, although it seemed like half an hour. When finally she finished a long, dirty, involved story of sexual sins, she breathed in a great amount of air, exhaled it, and slumped deep into her chair as if a burden had suddenly been lifted from her shoulders.

In the hushed silence that followed her confession, I asked her quietly if she had told this story to anyone else. She said, "No, and it has been hell on the inside for three years."

I began to explain to her the meaning of guilt, pointing out the difference between subjective, phony, personally imposed guilt, and the genuine, objective, lawful guilt that comes as God's norms in human nature are contradicted. I explained the finished work of our Lord on the cross. We had an exchange of questions and answers and a helpful discussion on how sin is washed away. When we finished talking and praying together, she showed great signs of relief plus a new optimism about herself. She left on a positive note.

I heard no more from the student or the superintendent of nurses until some weeks later when I got a phone call. The superintendent on the other end of the wire said, "I do not know what magic buttons you have on your desk, but I hope you keep them handy. I have never seen such change in a student. She is over her unprovoked crying spells. She has made peace with her roommate. She can concentrate in productive periods of study, and she got a good grade on her latest examination. I believe we can keep her, and she will graduate to become a good nurse." I responded in a noncommittal way by saying, "Sometimes you win and sometimes you lose." And I never told her of the student's problem of unconfessed sin.

I am a great believer in confession both theologically and psychologically. When David sought relief from the burning guilt heaped on him from his torrid affair with Bathsheba, his way back was through confession. His return to righteousness through (1) confession, (2) acceptance of personal responsibility, and (3) commitment to loving service is a pattern for us all.

Restitution

Restitution is an old-fashioned word, almost as unpopular as sin. According to the dictionary, restitution is "an act of restoring . . . . A restoration of something to its rightful owner . . . . making good, or giving an equivalent for some injury." In the days when life was simple, in agrarian America, stealing was usually related to tangibles such as hand tools, watermelons, and chickens. Most of the stealing was done by drifters or was just petty larceny among neighbors and store keepers. No one felt a need to lock their doors at night. Cattle rustlers and train robbers were members of gangs who lived in the hills or across the border. They belonged to a different category of humans. But among neighbors, restitution was a straightforward matter.

Things are different now. Life is complicated with divorce settlements, faceless corporations, legal departments, accounting procedures, white collar crime, gangs, irresponsible vandalism by youths, war crimes, valueless education, and a general breakdown in moral standards. It is not as easy now as it once was for pastors to preach on restitution. For instance, an effort to confess a series of lies about adultery when a divorce has already been finalized and both parties are remarried is not simple—and it might churn up more new problems than it resolves. If a person confesses his own part in a crime within the corporation, the confession is likely to reflect on other parties including both the guilty and the innocent. I went with a man to return hand tools to several corporate foundries where he had worked. Some personnel supervisors welcomed the idea while others were visibly shaken and confused. They did not know what to do with the man or his tools. Restitution today is primarily a matter for the courts. The most popular idea is to sue the person or the corporation who did you wrong and get what you can. If you are a defendant, plead innocent. If you have a good lawyer and are good at stonewalling you may get off with no restitution, in which case, consider yourself fortunate. It's a different world out there from what it used to be in small town U.S.A.

Against the backdrop of these and many more complicating factors, some people have decided restitution is not an important concern. This easy solution is a defense against their feelings of guilt. Many pastors have downplayed the idea of restitution and many laymen don't worry about it anymore.

I concede to all these problems related to restitution. But I still believe restitution is an important step in developing the habit of happiness. Talk with people who have gone through the painful process of restitution and let them tell you how it feels to get the monkey off your back. Several times each academic year I get letters from former students and alumni, some in high places, who are taking the final step in ridding themselves of guilt by confessing what they did in college. I have often read these letters and wondered in silence how long somebody's mind was troubled and torn before they decided to confess and make restitution. I have a special fund in the business office where restitution money is deposited to be used later to aid a worthy student.

During a week of chapel messages in a Canadian college, I must have touched the open nerve of unconfessed sin in a young theological student. Three weeks later I got an unusual letter. A student said he had listened to me each day and had come to the end of the series by making a difficult personal decision. Apparently he had been involved in some devious behavior years before, which brought a dark cloud over his sense of self-worth and left him with a load of guilt. His decision to prepare for the ministry was a move to get rid of his guilt. He was sure no minister could ever feel guilty, and therefore, if he became a minister the guilt would go away. He knew God had forgiven him but he could not forgive himself. For him, restitution was the only way he could be purged.

After I left the campus this theological student borrowed the money and flew home to eastern Canada where he did what he described as "the hardest thing of my life." He went to the people whom he had wronged and made confession, being well aware that coming forward might result in legal charges. However, the people in the company he had wronged were not interested in retaliation and graciously forgave him.

The exuberance of his spirit in this new-found freedom came through on every page of his long, hand-written letter.

And now the years rolled by. I went to Winona Lake, Indiana, to speak in a pastors' and wives' conference. I started up the tall steps to the old wooden hotel porch, a large case in each hand. Standing at the top of the steps was a young man grinning from ear to ear. When I reached the high porch, he said, "Let me take those suitcases. I want to carry them for you." (I don't know why he could not have made his offer while I was at the bottom of the steps.) He carried my suitcases through the lobby of the hotel knowing precisely where my room was assigned. I realized he had made advance arrangements to take me to my room. After he deposited the cases at the foot of the bed, the young preacher turned to me and asked, "Do you remember me?" Seeing the blank look on my face, he continued, "Do you remember receiving a letter from a Canadian student?"

I said, "Yes, I not only remember it, I still have the letter. It is among my keepsakes."

Then he went on to tell me, "I am the theology student who wrote you the letter."

At dinner that night I asked a neighboring pastor how things were going in the church where this young man was serving. With a smile of affirmation the minister said, "That young pastor has really got his life put together. He is at peace with everybody including himself. His church is growing, and he has a happy, helpful ministry." I did not tell the pastor why I had asked the question. I just responded by saying, "That is terrific." And it is terrific, any day we make a decision to face the problem of unconfessed sin in our lives.

There are reasons why people are slow to confess sin. Psychologists have made it clear that the inborn prosecutor is never satisfied until he has exacted out the last ounce of punishment for any norm that has been contradicted in human nature. Sometimes the consequences of sin show up in psychosomatic illness, in broken relationships, in low self-esteem, in feelings of rejection, and in loneliness. If the consequences are certain, then why do we hold on to sin rather than confess it and make it right?

(1) It is difficult to acknowledge weakness in ourselves. It is much easier to believe "everybody is doing it" than to acknowledge personal responsibility.

(2) We all face the fear of confession. *Maybe I will be stronger and think more of myself if I can stonewall it and never admit guilt. Maybe the confession won't do any good. Or, I'll just confess to God. He's forgiving. I don't need to face other people to get God's forgiveness.*

(3) And there is always concern for consequences. *If I confess wrong doing, the punishment may be something I don't want.*

(4) *If I wait long enough, the feelings of guilt may go away.* But for those who are able to go the way of confession and restitution there are the rewards of a clean slate, the repair of a tarnished relationship, and a quantum leap in self-esteem. Through restitution we have forgiven ourselves.

Discussion Questions:

1. Why is sin both actions and attitude?
2. How is sin an attitude?
3. What does confession mean to you?
4. Why is restitution always difficult?
5. What is the dictionary definition of restitution?

Wherefore gird up the loins of your mind, be sober, and hope to the end for the grace that is to be brought unto you at the revelation of Jesus Christ; as obedient children, not fashioning ourselves according to the former lusts in your ignorance: But as he which hath called you is holy, so be ye holy in all manner of conversation; Because it is written, Be ye holy; for I am holy (1 Peter 1:13–16).

Dearly beloved, I beseech you as strangers and pilgrims, abstain from fleshly lusts, which war against the soul; Having your conversation honest among the Gentiles; that, whereas they speak against you as evil-doers, they may by your good works, which they shall behold, glorify God in the day of visitation. Submit yourselves to every ordinance of man for the Lord's sake (1 Peter 2:11–13).

For he that will love life, and see good days, let him refrain his tongue from evil, and his lips that they speak no guile: let him eschew evil, and do good; let him seek peace, and ensue it (1 Peter 3:10–11).

And beside this, giving all diligence, add to your faith virtue; and to virtue knowledge; and to knowledge temperance; and to temperance patience; and to patience godliness; and to godliness brotherly kindness; and to brotherly kindness charity. For if these things be in you, and abound, they make you that ye shall neither be barren nor unfruitful in the knowledge of our Lord Jesus Christ. But he that lacketh these things is blind, and cannot see afar off, and hath forgotten that he was purged from his old sins. Wherefore the rather, brethren, give diligence to make your calling and election sure: for if ye do these things, ye shall never fall: For so an entrance shall be ministered unto you abundantly into the everlasting kingdom of our Lord and Savior Jesus Christ (2 Peter 1:5–11).

Habit is overcome by habit.

Thomas à Kempis

12

Our Attitude of Continuing Regard

Before moving on, let's take time for a progress report on how our attitudes can make or break our lives. (1) It is no accident that some people seem to get the good breaks in amazing ways while other people, who are just as good and seemingly just as deserving, continue to be the objects of disheartening problems beyond their control. (2) One answer to this syndrome of good luck or bad luck is related to the basic norms or laws God has built into human nature. (3) When we develop thought patterns (attitudes) that help us function in harmony with these inner laws, our lives move toward fulfillment and the habit of happiness. (4) If we develop thought patterns (attitudes) that go against this inner wisdom of the spirit the consequences show up in all the negative ways life can be experienced, including psychosomatic illnesses, broken relationships, bad marriages, shattered dreams of a successful career, and the general constriction of life. The wages of sin is death to all we might have been in this life and in the life to come.

Some Basic Steps

Since attitudes are learned responses they can be un-learned. Since attitudes are developed over a period of years they can be dismantled and replaced. No one needs to be without hope. The habit of happiness is within reach. Although the tyranny of the formula can often be a frustrating oversimplification, there are some basic steps we need to understand in our program for dealing with attitudes that are working against us instead of for us: (1) As far as possible, we need to trace our negative attitudes to their source. (2) We need to find a nonjudgmental person to talk with about our bad attitudes. (3) We need to commit our bad attitudes to God, fully. Don't try to consecrate them; get rid of them. (4) We can expect God to help us replace our negative attitudes with a new habit of happiness, which affirms life and gives us room to grow and develop. We cannot fall into the trap of being a passive seeker who expects God to relieve us of all responsibility by pushing one of his miracle buttons. Birth is a struggle and growing is a lifetime process. Don't try it by yourself. And don't expect God to do it all without you. God will help you develop the habit of happiness.

My short list of problem areas in the development of affirming attitudes is not exhaustive. But these four areas are of central concern for those who are serious about developing the habit of happiness.

(1) Facing up to the unresolved problem of resentment within us is a good point of departure. Healing in this area can bring dramatic results.

(2) Self-pity often grows out of resentment and can be the result of feeling victimized. Self-pity is to self-confidence what hostility is to gratitude. We can have one or the other but not both.

(3) Every unconfessed sin begins as a thought. And the habit of sinful thoughts is a way of describing depraved attitudes. The most depraved person is the one whose mind is most fully dominated by the habit of sinful thoughts. The

forgiveness and cleansing of sin is God's work. But two human factors are significant in forgiving ourselves: (a) confession and (b) restitution.

(4) This brings us to the fourth area which is troublesome in developing the habit of happiness:

Our Attitude of Continuing Regard

Our attitude of continuing regard is the predictable way we respond to events in our lives. Events come and go with the ebb and flow of life but our attitude of continuing regard tends to remain constant. Our friends know how we reacted in a given situation without having been there. "I'll bet he gave them a piece of his mind." If it turns out we did not give someone a piece of our mind our friends shake their heads slowly and say, "That's strange, it's not like him."

This attitude of continuing regard is not something we are born with. Attitudes are developed in the mind, not in the genes and stored. This basic set of attitudes we use for facing life develops in several ways:

(1) A lot of what we are is shaped by the culture in which we were born. A teenager who has grown up in Soweto near Johannesburg will have different attitudes toward democracy than a teenager who grew up in the town meetings of New England.

(2) The family value system has much to do with the development of the basic attitudes we use for coping with life. A teenager from a blue-collar home near a factory in Michigan will not look at life the same way a young adult does who developed his basic values and attitudes in a performing family of actors and actresses in Beverly Hills. Studies show that children raised in parsonages have greater academic success than children in the general population. Family values do matter.

(3) The relationship of a child with a significant person outside or inside his extended family such as a pastor, school teacher, parent, or relative can have a lasting effect on the

development of attitudes. I once asked a professor in the Business School of Harvard how he ever broke out of the cultural cocoon of a coal miner's home in a town of 200 people in western Pennsylvania. He finally became a national authority on labor relations and a full professor at Harvard. I might have anticipated his answer. He said, "It was a teacher in high school who took a special interest in me and made me believe I could do something really good with my life. He even got me the scholarship I needed to go to the University of Pennsylvania instead of getting a job at the mine."

However, the culture into which we were born, the family we were raised in, and the significant person in our lives are not the ultimate determinants of our attitude of continuing regard. All of us have the wide-open option of choosing the ways we will cope with life. The pattern of attitudes we develop may be greatly influenced by the culture, the family, and the significant person in our lives; but the attitudes we finally choose to live by are internalized as our own.

Let me say it again: The power of the culture, the influence of the home, and the impact of the significant person in our lives is hard to overstate. But the most important person in determining our attitude of continuing regard is ourselves. This is why there is always hope. Since we had a determining hand in making our attitudes what they are, we can, with the help of God, change them. The habit of happiness need not be an illusionary dream.

Two Basic Attitudes

The people of the world are divided into two camps when it comes to their attitude of continuing regard: those who are positive and those who are negative. By force of habit, each of us is either basically positive or basically negative. The negative person defends his attitudes with the rationale of being realistic while the positive person looks beyond the current state of affairs and sees people and situations in terms of possibilities.

The positive person puts things in their best light, allows people to be human, and does not judge everyone by a perfectionist standard. The negative person makes himself the judge and jury on the inevitable shortcomings in every situation. His conversation becomes a negative commentary on life. The person or the situation is the same for both negative and positive people, only their interpretations differ.

For years our family lived in the Williamette Valley of Oregon, a beautiful place filled with lush green foliage, bright flowers, and productive fields, all hedged by ranges of mountains capped with snow. But in Oregon it rains a lot. Oregonians do not particularly complain. First, the rain does not need to be shoveled like the snow back East. Second, it is the rain that makes the country unbelievably beautiful. And third, one day of gorgeous sunshine on snow-capped Mt. Hood and the ridges of the Cascade Mountains, and a native Oregonian will forgive the weatherman for all of his sins of prolonged wind and rain.

But for some people, this rainy condition is unforgivable. I have known people who were transferred to Portland and just couldn't take it. They finally quit their job and moved away because they could not accept the wet winter weather. Some people would rather have the desert and sunshine than the lush valleys and snow-capped mountains with their inevitable precipitation. Two people wrote letters from Portland, Oregon, to relatives back East on the very same day. One of them wrote, "It is a *beautiful day* in Oregon," while the other one said, "It is the *first day the sun has shone in a month.*" And they both told the truth. It was a beautiful day in Oregon, but it was also the first time the sun had shone in thirty days. The negative person discounted the day of sunshine while the positive person rejoiced in its splendor.

Is a glass half-full or half-empty when the liquid stands at mid-point? The answer may be related to what is in the glass. A weary traveler on camel back in the Sahara Desert would view the mid-point of water supply in his canteen as half-empty. But the same mid-point in a glass of castor oil could be seen as half-full by a hospital patient.

I once worked hard in the promotion of a banquet held in the interest of a project many of us valued highly. While I was sitting at the head table looking over the banquet room, my heart was warmed by the sight of many couples whom I had urged to attend. I was feeling especially good about the response when the co-chairman leaned over to me and in a raspy, negative voice said, "Doc, I was just sitting here thinking about all the people who did not show."

And that's the way it is with life. The experiences ebb and flow as the days come and go, but our attitude of continuing regard either casts the events in a positive light or sets them in distorting shadows. While life flows on like a river, each of us decides to be positive or negative about what sails by.

Pandemonium reigned after Babe Ruth hit his second history-making home run in the famous game in Chicago; many say he gestured toward the outfield fence before he swung his bat, indicating where the ball would go. The players literally carried him around the bases, or at least part of the way, making it hard for him to touch the bags. More than twenty minutes passed before the umpires could clear away the debris of celebration from the field and settle down the players and fans to continue the game. It was only the fourth inning.

After the game was over the writers were having their inning in the locker room where they interviewed the Babe about the gesture of his bat toward the centerfield fence and his apparent intention to hit a home run. This was the story of the year destined to be retold and written about as long as people continued to love baseball. Just as they were concluding the interview, one sportswriter said, "Babe, I have just one more question to ask before we go. What would you have done if you had missed that third strike?" Babe Ruth's jaw dropped with the uninhibited expression of sincerity that comes when there is no premeditated response. And out popped his answer, "It never entered my mind to do anything but hit a home run."

Many negative people have already struck out before they leave the house on any working day. Their attitude of continuing regard is like a monster with many tentacles wrapped around the possibilities of their minds, holding them back from success, increasing their frustration, and making them failures. Positive people leave home for the ball park or the office expecting good things to happen. With them, the habit of happiness is standard equipment.

Discussion Questions:

1. Are attitudes learned responses?
2. If so, how can they be unlearned?
3. What is our attitude of continuing regard?
4. How does our attitude of continuing regard explain our successes and failures?

DR. LESLIE PARROTT is President of Olivet
Nazarene University in Kankakee, Illinois. He
earned his Ph.D at Michigan State University and
is an ordained minister in the Church of the
Nazarene. He was previously President of Eastern
Nazarene College in Quincy, Massachusetts. He
has pastored churches in Kelso, Washington;
Flint, Michigan; Kirkland, Washington; and
Portland, Oregon. *The Habit of Happiness* is his
tenth book. Dr. Parrott has done post-doctoral
work in educational management at Harvard
University.